T. D. JAKES

presents

*God's*
*Leading*
*Ladies*™

CONFERENCE
WORKBOOK

THOMAS NELSON PUBLISHERS®
Nashville

# T. D. JAKES
### presents

## God's Leading Ladies™

# CONFERENCE
# WORKBOOK

*Taking Your Place on Life's Center Stage*

## T.D. Jakes

THOMAS NELSON PUBLISHERS®
Nashville

Published by Thomas Nelson, Inc., P.O. Box 141000,
Nashville, Tennessee, 37214.

ISBN 0-7852-5040-9

Printed in Canada

03 04 05 06 07 — 5 4 3 2 1

# Contents

# Dear Leading Lady,

What a joy it is to be able to present you with this workbook! It is absolutely filled with practical information that will edify, and with truth that will transform! Becoming a leading lady is a process—it takes commitment, passion, and determination. But it also takes some education in terms of how to really live your life, day in and day out, as a leading lady. After all, God has entrusted you with much, and I believe you are eager to be a faithful steward and an effective manager of everything He has put in your hands—your relationships, your career, your finances, your health and appearance—all of the things that make you the confident, successful woman that you are! In this book, you will find three sections: one on relationships, one on finances, and one on health—all designed to help you to live "to the max." So grab a hot cup of coffee and a pen, maybe even your Bible and your journal if you wish, and get ready to be informed and equipped to be the very best leading lady you can possibly be!

In order to help you get started, I'd like to take a moment to walk you through each of the features you will find in the pages of this workbook so that you will understand why I have included them and what I hope your interaction with them will accomplish in your life.

*Introducing* . . . : The word speaks for itself. Introductions to each chapter will simply show you the big picture of the subject covered and give you a glimpse of where we are headed in that chapter.

*The Main Event* : I am delighted by the wealth of sound, practical advice and godly wisdom in this workbook. This helpful information is presented to you in sections entitled, "The Main Event," which is divided into "Acts," just as a play on the stage is divided into acts. Each act focuses specifically on a particular aspect of the larger subject of the chapter.

*You're On* : One of my hopes for you as you work through this book is that you will find all kinds of ways to apply its information to your own life. To help you in that purpose, I have included some questions for you to answer. I hope you'll think about them, answer them, and even use an extra sheet of paper or your journal if you find yourself wanting to think about them more thoroughly or answer them more extensively.

*Learn Your Lines* : You probably know that God's Word is "living and active," as we read in the Book of Hebrews, but I want you to continue to experience its transforming power in your daily life. Therefore, at the end of each "Act," you will find several scriptures to memorize in connection with the subject you have just studied. As the Word gets worked into your mind, it gets worked out in your life, so I believe these scriptures really are keys to help you unlock personal victory and success.

*Coming Soon* : I love this part of the workbook because it is your chance to dream on paper. These beautifully designed pages at the end of each chapter will allow you to write a synopsis of what you have learned in each chapter, to summarize how you will put those lessons into practice, and to take time to really think about your life and get your hopes, aspirations, and inspirations on paper.

*Action!* : Goal-setting is so important to successful living, and that is why I have included, at the conclusion of every chapter, a place for you to list specific goals pertaining to the topic of that chapter. I encourage you to use that space to set a few measurable, challenging-but-attainable goals, and to give yourself a deadline and a reward for reaching them. In the back of the workbook, you will find an Appendix in which you can put all of your goals together on one list and prioritize them.

God bless you!
T.D. Jakes

# Your Relationships

# 1

# The Leading Lady

## Introducing

There comes a time, I suppose, in every woman's life when she gives herself a "progress report." Some women evaluate themselves intentionally, while others stumble or slide into moments of reflection, but the same types of questions usually arise. "How have the years passed so quickly?" "Why didn't I do those things I longed to do?" "Will I ever fulfill my divine destiny?" "What happened to all those dreams that once burned inside of me?" And, last but not least, "Is it too late now?"

I can only answer the last question for you and say with all my might, "No! It isn't too late for you!" Whether you are 21 or 81, the rest of your life stretches out before you like an untraveled highway, and you have an opportunity to be God's leading lady for as long as your presence graces this earth.

Now when I write about being a leading lady, I simply mean that you can be everything God created you to be and that you can live a life of grand purpose and significance. Yes, you can fulfill your God-given destiny, maximize all of your glorious potential, and take your place in this world with your head held high.

I believe it's that time for you. Lady, you have worked hard and waited long; and now is your time to shine. In order to sparkle like you should, you are going to have to abandon your past, accept your present, and anticipate your future.

# The Main Event

## Act 1: Put Yesterday Behind You

One of the first decisions you must make if you are going to be a leading lady is to put the past behind you. I mean it. I understand how painful the past can be and how difficult letting go can be, but I also know that old memories and old wounds and old fears will cripple you if you do not deal with them and lay them to rest.

You must choose whether you want to live in yesterday's recollections or today's possibilities, because it really is impossible to do both. One of the marks of a leading lady is her ability to keep moving forward, no matter how the past attempts to stop her or to slow her down. She resolves what can be resolved and reconciles what can be reconciled. But she refuses to be haunted by the past, so she silences the whining of days gone by with a decisive act of her will. She simply makes up her mind to walk on.

## You're On

1. What are the most painful memories of your past?

Loss of relationships,
Missed opportunities
Being fat
Divorce

**2.** How have the things you listed above kept you from doing and being everything God has for you?

*The past grew me up too fast giving no time for spontaneous fun*

**3.** Are you willing to let go of your pain, even if your inner wounds have become a familiar friend or a part of your personality? *I want to be free from stinkin thinkin.*

**4.** <u>Pray</u> now and surrender every painful, shameful thing that has happened to you in the past. <u>Forgive</u> those who have hurt you and ask the Lord to <u>heal</u> your heart so that you can go forward, strong and whole.

> *I understand how painful the past can be and how difficult letting go can be, but I also know that old memories and old wounds and old fears will cripple you if you do not deal with them and lay them to rest.*

## *Learn Your Lines*

*Therefore if anyone is in Christ, he is a new creation; old things have passed away; behold, all things have become new.*

**2 Corinthians 5:17**

*Do not remember the former things, nor consider the things of old.*
*Behold, I will do a new thing, now it shall spring forth;*
*shall you not know it? I will even make a road in the wilderness*
*and rivers in the desert.*

**Isaiah 43:18, 19**

*As far as the east is from the west, so far has He removed*
*our transgressions from us.*

**Psalm 103:12**

## *Act 2: Embrace Today*

You have heard it said, "There's no time like the present!" and I want to assure you that those words are true. They are not only true; they are powerful if you will believe them and act on them. Although I wholeheartedly believe in God's perfect timing for certain events and specific breakthroughs, I am also aware that human nature is to procrastinate sometimes, especially when the challenge before us seems daunting.

I want to ask you a question that will help you determine how to live your life today and every day from now on. The only way to embrace the present is to find out what really matters to you, for that is the endeavor, the adventure, or the relationship to which you will devote your passion and your energy. So, leading lady, "What is it in your life that you are willing to fight for?"

Whatever is worth fighting for is worth living for right this minute, and I hope you will not let another day pass without reaching out for the prize. Time is passing, and lady, the drum is sounding. Can you hear it? It's thumping out the rhythm of your life and it is time for you to start

> *The only way to embrace the present is to find out what really matters to you, for that is the endeavor, the adventure or the relationship to which you will devote your passion and your energy.*

marching to its beat. Don't wait for something to jolt you into the reality that every passing day is a piece of your life—the life you have been given to maximize. Don't lose today by clinging to what is behind you, or by dreaming aimlessly about what you want for your future. <u>Use today and drain it dry!</u> Embrace the moments you have right now and invest them in all that you are and all that you will be!

## You're On

*1.* What are five wonderful things about the life you are living right now? Money is not a big worry
My home is looking more spa-like
I have strong friendships
I participate in Christian fellowship
Convertibles are year round cars.

*2.* What needs to be eliminated from your life so that you can fully and freely enjoy the present? How will you let go of those situations or relationships?
Extra hours @ work - How much time should I really spend working?
Schedule exercise by watching less TV
Be positive not negative. Model it for Jay

**3.** What difficult or painful aspects of your present are you hiding from, denying, or refusing to embrace? What attitude adjustments do you need to make in order to throw your arms around those things so that you can deal with them and move on?

My marriage isn't all I'd hope it would be. Losing weight during times of stress is next to impossible.
✱Everyday I can choose a better attitude, make healthier food/fitness choices

**4.** List five words that you would like to accurately describe the way you currently live? How can you incorporate those qualities into your life today?
Classy
Full
Prudent/Good Steward
Elegant
Adventure

## Learn Your Lines

*Arise, shine; for your light has come!*
*And the glory of the Lord is risen upon you!*

**Isaiah 60:1**

*This is the day the Lord has made;*
*we will rejoice and be glad in it.*
**Psalm 118:24**

*I have come that they might have life,*
*and that they might have it abundantly.*
**John 10:10**

## Act 3:  Look Toward Tomorrow

You understand what it means to look toward tomorrow, to behold within your soul that which cannot be seen by the natural eye, to have such a clear vision of the future that no situation, no employer, no friend, or foe can cloud it. You understand what happens on the horizon: you set your gaze upon the God-given dreams inside of you and they become larger and more defined as you move toward them. Lady, you are closer now than ever before to their fulfillment, so it is time to look closely so that you can be prepared to embrace them wisely and completely when they become reality.

When your dreams do begin to dawn on the landscape of your life, you will want to be prepared to embrace them, to manage them, to maintain them, and to grow them. Looking toward tomorrow may require you to do some things today so that you are ready for the greatness that awaits you. May I suggest just five key areas of your life you will want take a look at and make sure you are prepared for the future?

> *When your dreams do begin to dawn on the landscape of your life, you will want to be prepared to embrace them, to maintain them, and to grow them.*

*Finances*: Make sure that your financial affairs are in order and that you have the money you will need. So many dreams sink because of poor financial planning or because the dreamer underestimates the money she will need in order to succeed. Be wise and informed in regard to what you want to do, so that lack of finances will not cause failure.

*Relationships:* Perhaps your dream involves your family. Are those relationships everything they should be? Perhaps you will need an attorney or a CPA; go ahead and find the right people for your plan. Maybe you will need the support of your church family or people who are committed to praying for you daily; make sure you have that relational structure in place.

*Emotional and Spiritual Health*: Are you strong and stable emotionally? The realization of dreams and destiny can be intense and demanding. Just as giving birth to a child is physically grueling, giving birth to your future can be a high-pressure experience, both emotionally and spiritually. Deal with your issues and resolve them so that they do not rear their ugly heads when the heat is on, for they will. Feed yourself a steady diet of the Word and prayer and worship, so that your soul's energy comes from the never-ending, rich supply of the Spirit.

*Physical Fitness*: Whatever your dream is, it may involve long hours and/or physical labor. Make sure you are physically fit and strong so that you will have the energy to meet every demand. Make sure that you eat well and feed yourself the foods that will help you and not hinder you.

*Matters of Appearance*: Do you need a new wardrobe for your new role in life? If so, start building now. Do you need a make-over or a new haircut? Make those appointments so you will look like the leading lady that you are!

# *You're On*

*1.* Gaze into your own heart and look for hope. Does hope need to be rekindled in you? If so, jot a brief prayer in the space below and ask the Lord to stir hope in you again.

*Thank-you Lord for a Mom who modeled life for me. The pain of her death has caused me depression for which I know you are the cure. Heal me Lord, create a new, brave, joyful heart in me. May my joy be so full it spills into my home, family & friends.*

*2.* As you think about your future, what three virtues would you most like to develop?

*① Good steward of all God provides for me — time, food, finances.*

*② Grace, elegance & style as I age*

*③ A stronger prayer life*

*3.* What would you like to change about your routine or your approach to life? How can you begin to implement these changes?

*4³⁰ devotion*
*5 tread / yoga*
*5⁴⁵ shower*
*6³⁰ leave for work*
*4³⁰ go to gym (leave work)*
*6 dinner*

*Schedule and tell my family. Celebrate success*

*4.* Think about the woman you would like to be six months from today, one year from today, and five years from today? What words would you use to describe her?

*Faithful, fit, tucks shirts into jeans, someone I'd like to hang out with*

*5.* What practical steps of preparation do you need to take now in order to be ready when your dreams come to pass?

*Clean out closet*
*Plan fall shopping*
*Exercise*

## Learn Your Lines

*For I know the thoughts that I think toward you, says the Lord, thoughts of peace and not of evil, to give you a future and a hope.*

**Jeremiah 29:11**

*. . . He who has begun a good work in you will complete it . . .*

**Philippians 1:6**

*. . . I press on, that I may lay hold of that for which Christ Jesus has also laid hold of me. Brethren, I do not count myself to have apprehended; but one thing I do, forgetting those things which are behind me and reaching forward to those things which are ahead, I press toward the goal for the prize of the upward call of God in Christ Jesus.*

**Philippians 3:12–14**

# COMING SOON

*L*ady, there are hopes and dreams inside of you and it is time for you to dream again. Maybe they have been buried beneath layers of pain, shame, or disappointment and are just now beginning to be unearthed as you have released the pain of your past in this chapter. Maybe they are pushing against your mind like a racehorse ready to burst through the starting gate. Whatever your situation, I invite you to put your dreams on paper in the space provided. Write about what you hope for as you think of your life, what you long to accomplish, or the pleasures you want to experience and enjoy. This is your life we are talking about, so let your thoughts run wild!

My house is paid off early so I can retire @ 60 instead of 65. I'm fit because I take time to take care of myself. Jay & I travel where he can meet people and I can exercise. I have a regular spa I go to in my community and maintain a hair style. Seeing the world through Worldmark takes me on many adventures and I realize the benefits of flying 1st class on long flights over the ocean.

# ACTION!

*B*ased on what you have learned in this chapter, what are three concise, measurable, attainable goals you will set for yourself as a leading lady? Be sure to include a schedule and target date for reaching each goal and a reward for accomplishing it.

1. Goal: *Right weight*
   Schedule and target completion date: *30 weeks*
   Reward: *Spa day w/ 3 treatments*

2. Goal: *Debt free—sons house*
   Schedule and target completion date: *5 yrs.*
   Reward: *Pay cash for SUV*

3. Goal: *CTE credentials for Admin*
   Schedule and target completion date: *Fall 2012*
   Reward: *out of classroom*

# 2

# The Lady and Her Lord

## Introducing

Every little girl longs for a father, and every leading lady needs one, too. The good news is that, regardless of the relationship you have or had with your earthly dad, you have a heavenly Father who loves you perfectly, guides you with impeccable wisdom, and cheers you on every step of the way. There is no foundation as firm as the love of God and no refuge as safe. There is no balm as healing and no zeal as fervent. He loved you and knew you before you were even formed in your mother's womb and from the beginning of time, He has had a wonderful plan for your life, and He dreams bigger dreams for you than you can envision for yourself.

The lady who lives her life in His presence is unstoppable. As you take your place on life's center stage, the Lord is the only director whose cues you can fully trust!

# *The Main Event*

## *Act 1: Knowing Him*

There is no relationship on earth so pure, so intimate, so tender, so powerful, and so deeply satisfying as the relationship between a person and the Lord. All true success in life begins and ends with knowing the Lord and enjoying a vibrant, faith-filled, heart-to-heart relationship with Him.

> *There is no relationship on earth so pure, so intimate, so tender, so powerful, and so deeply satisfying as the relationship between a person and the Lord.*

He is the one who created you, He thinks you are exquisite. He is the one who fashioned your heart, and He knows its deepest longings. He is the one who calms your fears and dries your tears and gives you the courage to go on. He fuels your fire, fulfills your desire, and calls you to places of greatness you cannot even imagine.

The best way to get to know Him is through His Word, the Bible. Perhaps you have grown up knowing the Scriptures, and perhaps you have not. If you are not acquainted with God's Word, please get to know this marvelous Book. There are so many translations available today, some in contemporary language that is easy to understand and some that maintain the grandeur of more traditional wording.

Whatever approach you would like to take to the Scriptures, I encourage you to get out your Bible and read. Read not for the purpose of gaining historical or theological knowledge, but for the purpose of knowing the God who made you and who directs your life and who loves you with an everlasting love. Listed below are just some of the countless places in Scripture where you will find wonderful insight into who God is, so that you might know Him more intimately.

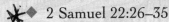

- ✳ Exodus 15:26 (last sentence of the verse)
- ✦ Deuteronomy 30:9, 10
- ✳ 2 Samuel 22:26–35
- ✳ Joshua 1:5–9
- ✦ Psalm 3:3; 18:2; 27:1; 30:1–3; 33:18; 57:2; 65:2; 84:11; 97:10; 113:7–9
- ✦ Isaiah 50:7–9; 54:4–10; 58:9; 64:8
- ✦ Jeremiah 31:3; 33:6
- ✦ The Gospel of John
- ✳ Romans 8:37–39
- ✦ Ephesians 2:14–18
- ✦ 1 Timothy 1:14, 15
- ✦ Hebrews 4:15, 16

> *He is the one who created you, He thinks you are exquisite.*

## You're On

*1.* What words would you use to describe God? Do your thoughts about Him reflect who His Word says He is? Yes

*Omni-everything, Father, Lord, Deliverer*

*2.* After you have read the Scriptures in the list, choose several that are especially meaningful to you, Based on the Scriptures you chose, what is God really like? *He adores me as I adore Him.*

**3.** Do you believe God loves you personally and passionately? Do you believe that He is constantly working for your good? If so, hallelujah! If not, ask Him now to begin to reveal His love and to begin to share His heart for you.

*He is working for me – a labor of His love.*

**4.** On a scale of 1–10, how well do you think you know God? If you long to know Him more accurately, in the space provided, write a brief prayer from your heart and ask Him to reveal Himself to you.

*8*

*Help me to know you better Lord. Encourage me as I try to grow in my faith with you*

## *Learn Your Lines*

*. . . God is love.*

**1 John 4:8**

*The Lord your God in your midst, the Mighty One, will save;*
*He will rejoice over you with gladness, He will quiet you with His love,*
*He will rejoice over you with singing.*

**Zephaniah 3:17**

*. . . but the people who know their God shall be strong,*
*and carry out exploits.*

**Daniel 11:32**

*For I am the Lord, I do not change . . .*
**Malachi 3:6**

## Act 2: Trusting Him

I'd like to share a story with you, a story about a young woman who lived centuries ago, a young woman whose life reveals the truths of trust perhaps better than anything else I could recount to you. Perhaps you know her story, but you may understand it from a different perspective today. Perhaps you know her name, but she may become more alive today as you identify with her courage as she submitted herself entirely to the will of God. We only knew her first name—Mary. But when that is followed by "the mother of Jesus," I suppose one name is more than enough!

She was so very young and so very pure. She was the earthly vessel through whom God chose to send His son to earth, and she was brimming with dedication to His holy purposes and faith in His holy promise. No doubt she had plans and dreams of her own regarding her future, but when God asked her to embrace a different destiny, the ultimate leading lady role, she turned away from everything else and said, "Behold, the maidservant of the Lord! Let it be to me according to your word" (Luke 1:38). She agreed to all the uncertainties of having a baby—the physical changes, the emotional ups and downs, the enormous responsibilities. And she did so knowing that she could be left alone for the rest of her life, that Joseph, her fiancé, might duck and run when he found her pregnant. But Mary knew beyond a shadow of a doubt that the Lord had chosen her and she responded by believing His word and singing His praises. I can't think of a better example of trust.

*Her greatness was born the instant she pushed fear aside, silenced her wonderings, and said yes to the Father.*

Learn the lessons of trusting God from this young woman who lived so long ago, a lady whose entire destiny depended on her willingness to release all of her own plans into the purposes of God, a lady who has been, and is, honored through the ages. Remember that Mary faced an unnerving situation—the ridicule of those around her and the possible loss of the man she loved. But her greatness was born the instant she pushed fear aside, silenced her wonderings, and said yes to the Father. And, that, leading lady, is the essence of trusting the God who is so much greater than you are.

## You're On

1. How are you doing in the area of trusting God? If you are not trusting Him, how is being in charge of your own life going?

*I trust Him but with reservations. This is not what He wants - complete trust is the only way to "get out of the boat"*

2. Who in your past has proven untrustworthy and has therefore caused you to be afraid to trust God?

*Most of my brothers & sisters, I haven't kept promises, my sons, Jay, My Dad*

**3.** List three specific areas of your heart or aspects of your life situations that you need to trust and release to the Lord.

*Love,*
*Listening to Jay*
*Wellness esp weight related issues*

**4.** If you find it hard to trust, use the space provided to write a brief prayer asking God to help you.

*I trust myself but Lord I need to extend that trust to others. Help me Lord towards better responses regarding trust*

## *Learn Your Lines*

*Trust in the Lord with all your heart, and lean not*
*on your own understanding; in all your ways acknowledge Him,*
*and He shall direct your paths.*

**Proverbs 3:5, 6**

*As for God, His way is perfect; the word of the Lord is proven;*
*He is a shield to all who trust in Him.*

**1 Samuel 22:31**

*The Lord is good, a stronghold in the day of trouble;*
*and He knows those who trust in Him.*

**Nahum 1:7**

*And know in all your hearts and all your souls that not one thing has*
*failed of all the good things which the Lord your God spoke concerning*
*you. All have come to pass for you; not one word of them has failed.*

**Joshua 23:14**

## Act 3: Serving Him

What do you think of when you consider what it means to serve God? Perhaps you think of preachers or nuns or missionaries in the far corners of the earth. All of those people are indeed servants of God. But so are the university professors, the physicians, the computer analysts, the florists, the architects, the newscasters, the travel agents, and the CEOs of major corporations. Lady, whatever you choose to do is to be done as unto the Lord. And whatever you choose to do can be offered up to Him as a holy sacrifice. You may be called into the ministry. You may be the one He has called to spread His fame throughout the world of sports or entertainment or the media. You may be the one appointed to pray for divine healing as you attend to your patients. You may be the one to advance His kingdom in the financial empires of this world. Wherever He has placed you and in whatever arena He has gifted you to excel, that is your place of service unto Him.

> *Wherever He has placed you and in whatever arena He has gifted you to excel, that is your place of service unto Him.*

# *You're On*

*1.* Do you understand that serving God is a matter of the heart and not a function of your behavior? Absolutely

*2.* In what areas of your life are you trying to serve God out of a sense of obligation, guilt, fear, or a desire to impress people or please Him?

organized missional service @ church

*3.* If serving God is based in any of the feelings in question 2, are you willing to quit performing long enough to get established in God so that you can then serve Him in the right ways and with the right motivation?

Shutting down is the best way to reboot who I am in Jesus.

> If you are going to be successful in life and in all of the things that compose your life, you will need to be able to hear God's voice so that you can follow Him into all of the wonderful places He leads. But in order to hear His voice, you must know Him.

*4.* When your service to God is rooted in a passion for Him, how can you serve God in areas of your life that may not seem "religious"—on your job, in your home, on a shopping trip, at lunch with friends?

Taking the time & energy to make deeper relationships - that means taking risks. w/my feelings.

# *Learn Your Lines*

*And now, Israel, what does the Lord require of you, but to fear the Lord your God, to walk in all His ways and to love Him, to serve the Lord your God with all your heart and with all your soul.*

**Deuteronomy 10:12**

*But now we have been delivered from the law, having died to what we were held by, so that we should serve in the newness of the Spirit and not in the oldness of the letter.*

**Romans 7:6**

*And whatever you do, do it heartily, as to the Lord and not to men, knowing that from the Lord you will receive the reward of the inheritance; for you serve the Lord Christ.*

**Colossians 3:23, 24**

# COMING SOON

$\mathscr{L}$ady, the Lord is leading you in more ways than you can even imagine. The God who loves you has plans for you; He has filled your life with purpose and your future with more goodness and excitement than you have believed possible. As you think about your personal relationship with Him, what is it that you long to experience? How deeply in love do you want to fall with your Lord? What do you want to know about Him? How do you want to grow in your understanding of His love, in your prayer life, or in the ways you trust and serve Him? What is on your spiritual horizon?

Become more aware of heaven and the legacy my mom left me. Engage in a fulfilling prayer life with others and God. Enjoy being 50 and beyond esp. living a full life into my 90's.

# ACTION!

*B*ased on what you have learned in this chapter, what are three concise, measurable, attainable goals you will set for yourself in your relationship with the Lord? Be sure to include a schedule and target date for reaching each goal and a reward for accomplishing it.

*1.* Goal:
   Schedule and target completion date:
   Reward:

*2.* Goal:
   Schedule and target completion date:
   Reward:

*3.* Goal:
   Schedule and target completion date:
   Reward:

# 3

# The Lady on Her Own

## Introducing

In the course of my ministry, I have observed many, many single women and learned that, at the end of the day, a single woman can be extremely pitiful or intensely powerful. Often, the journey from pity to power is a slow process consisting of questions and confusion, unmet expectations, cycles of desperation and tough resolve, the pain of lost love, and the liberating experience of finally seeing yourself for who you are and embracing the wonderful life that is yours, whether it includes a man or not. If you are a true leading lady and are single for any reason, you may have already discovered how powerful your life as a single woman can be. In this chapter, I want to celebrate that with you.

# The Main Event

## Act 1: The Sensational Single

When God calls a woman to be single, whether she is single for a season or single for a lifetime, one of the greatest gifts He gives her is freedom. And the most successful single women I know are the ones who embrace and rejoice in and maximize the liberty of their lives. If you are single, now is your moment. You are free to live any way you want to. The spotlight is on you and it is time for you to shine. Your time is yours; your money is yours; your energy is yours; your creativity is yours—and you are free to use all of those commodities any way you wish. If you are responsible for children or for the elderly, those responsibilities may limit some aspects of your freedom, but it does not diminish your power. When you shape and guide young lives, that is the power of influence! When you honor the aged by caring for them, that is the power of love. Nevertheless, God has a plan for you that only you can accomplish, and He knows how to enable you to accomplish it, regardless of your responsibilities.

I cannot tell you what to do with your life. I can only tell you that much of your potential for power comes from the freedom of your state as an unmarried woman. Your life can be sensational because you are free to live it without consulting anyone but the Spirit of the living God. And, lady, the Spirit of God does not have any unresolved issues; He does not bring to your relationship the baggage of the past; He does not compare you with a former girlfriend (or a mother!), and everything He does is in your best interest and comes from a heart of pure, passionate, holy love for you. When you are single, He is the only One you need to partner with!

> *The most successful single women I know are the ones who embrace and rejoice in and maximize the liberty of their lives.*

Now is your moment unlike any other. You are healed; you are strong; you are whole. And you are free to impact the world. I challenge you to use the pleasures and privileges of your singleness to the benefit of yourself, to the service of those around you, and to the maximum glory of the God who has gifted you with the power to live a sensational life!

## *You're On*

*1.* Are you living a sensational single life? If not, how can you begin to do so?

*2.* What wonderful and unique opportunities do you have because you are single?

*3.* How can you use the fact that you are single to help or serve someone else?

*4.* Have you fully embraced the fact that you are single? Do you feel loved and accepted by God and others? If not, jot down a brief prayer in the space below and ask God to help you understand how sensational you can be.

*5.* Where is your greatest potential for power and how can you maximize it?

## *Learn Your Lines*

*There is a difference between a wife and a virgin. The unmarried woman cares about the things of the Lord, that she may be holy, both in body and spirit. But she who is married cares about the things of the world—how she may please her husband. And this I say for your own profit, not that I may put a leash on you, but for what is proper, and that you may serve the Lord without distraction.*

**1 Corinthians 7:34, 35**

*Not that I speak in regard to need, for I have learned in whatever state
I am, to be content: I know how to be abased, and I know how to
abound. Everywhere and in all things I have learned both to be full and
to be hungry, both to abound and to suffer need. I can do all things
through Christ who strengthens me.*

**Philippians 4:11–13**

*The lines have fallen to me in pleasant places; yes,
I have a good inheritance.*

**Psalm 16:6**

## *Act 2: Celebrating You*

One of the great gifts of singleness is that you are free to spend
your time and your money to celebrate and pamper yourself. I
encourage you to do so with joy, with creativity, and with
regularity. Below are several suggestions, in a variety
of price ranges, to help you get started.

◆ Surround your bathtub with candles and fill
it with bubbles. Turn the lights off and
bask in the soft glow as you soak in the
warmth of the bath.

◆ Write a book that celebrates who you are
by getting a new journal and filling it with
stories of your life, with quotations, and
Bible verses that are meaningful to you,
with your hopes and dreams.

◆ Have your portrait taken. Frame it nicely for
yourself; give prints to people you love.

◆ Buy yourself a new outfit that looks fabulous on you.

*One
of the great
gifts of singleness
is that you are free
to spend your time
and your money to
celebrate and
pamper yourself.*

◆ Spend a day at the spa. Order the services that seem most luxurious to you.

◆ Spend a weekend at a hotel. Treat yourself like a star.

◆ Look at your bedroom. Is it the kind of room that befits a woman of your quality and tastes? If not, redecorate if you can afford to. If not, plan what you would like to do, get one item that will inspire you to continue the project, and budget for the rest. As you can, do this throughout the place you live.

◆ Take yourself out for ice cream.

◆ Order your favorite meal from your favorite restaurant and eat at home by candlelight on your finest china.

◆ Overcome an obstacle.

◆ Worship God with passion and extravagance in the privacy of your own home.

◆ Read that book you haven't taken time to read.

◆ Map the goodness of the Lord through your life by remembering and tracing His blessings through the years. Think about how perfect His plan has been, how things have worked together for your good, how impeccable His timing has been, how He has brought the right people into your life at precisely the right moment, etc. Draw these things on a map or write them down.

◆ Do something creative.

◆ Give something only you can give—or in that special way that only you can give it—to someone else.

◆ Get quiet and ask the Lord how He sees you. Listen to what He says. I guarantee a celebration when you hear His response!

◆ Plant a tree in honor of yourself.

◆ Don't just pour yourself a cup of coffee in the mornings, learn to make a great latte or whatever it is that you like.

◆ Work on your signature look or choose your signature fragrance. (More on this in chapter 17).

◆ On a day you do not have to report to work, don't set the alarm.

## *You're On*

*1.* What is the most wonderful thing about you?

*2.* When was the last time you did something really special for yourself? What are three things you could do to celebrate yourself this week?

*3.* You know from Zephaniah 3:17 that the Lord rejoices over you with singing. What do you think He would like to say to you as He celebrates the woman He has made in you?

# *Learn Your Lines*

*I have come that they may have life,*
*and that they may have it more abundantly.*
**John 10:10**

*Rejoice in the Lord always. Again I will say, rejoice!*
**Philippians 4:4**

*You will show me the path of life; in Your presence is fullness of joy;*
*at Your right hand are pleasures forevermore.*
**Psalm 16:11**

*And my soul shall be joyful in the Lord;*
*it shall rejoice in His salvation.*
**Psalm 35:9**

## *Act 3: So You Want to Be a Wife?*

Over the course of many years as a pastor, I have met more than a few single women whose single purpose in life seems to be finding a husband. So many times, these women end up ignoring wise counsel and making fools of themselves as they run around in hot pursuit of any decent human being of the male gender!

I want to say to you that there is absolutely nothing wrong with wanting to fall in love and get married. The desire to be a wife is healthy and holy when it is properly aligned with God's plan and timing for your life. Between now and the time that right man does come along, there are some simple things you can do to make sure that you are prepared to love him well.

> *The desire to be a wife is healthy and holy when it is properly aligned with God's plan and timing for your life.*

First, if there is any anxiety or sense of urgency in your heart about getting married, cool it. Not everyone is called to be married, but many women are. Settle the issue with the Lord in the privacy of your own heart. Discover His will for you in this area and move toward peaceful acceptance of it. If you believe that marriage is God's highest and best for you, ask Him to forgive you for trying to take charge of your life, because He is the one who is in control of everything and He really does know what is best for you. Tell Him that you submit to His timing and His grace in this area of your life. Tell Him that you want the man He has chosen for you and that you will not settle for less. Then go one step further and begin to thank Him for bringing His wonderful will to pass in a way that will blow your mind!

Take an honest look at yourself and evaluate your strengths and weaknesses. You want to be healed and whole and strong as you enter a relationship, so deal with your insecurities, your interpersonal skills, your neediness, and your fears or misconceptions about men and relationships. There are many books and resources available to help you gain a better understanding of the opposite sex and to help you learn the fine art of relating to a man. I know there are some things we must "learn by doing," but I really encourage you to educate yourself in this regard as thoroughly as possible.

Finally, prepare yourself in the arena of money. Start by getting out of debt, because I can assure you that there is no man on earth who wants to bail you out financially!

> *Dating requires that you spend time together to get to know the person — brief, frequent encounters over a prolonged period. Avoid concentrations of time, such as entire days spent together when you first begin dating. You need time to process the information you gain about a person.*

What I have shared in the paragraphs above is by no means comprehensive. In fact, it just scratches the surface. But, I trust that it will help you and I believe that it does point you in the right direction to continue down a solid path toward your future as you prepare to be an excellent wife someday.

## *You're On*

*1.* Look at yourself objectively and not out of your desires or emotions. Do you really believe you are ready to share your life with a man?

*2.* How are you going to make the most of the time you have left as a single woman?

*3.* What are three ways you can be a blessing to your husband when he comes?

*4.* What do you think are the most significant works of healing and wholeness the Lord has done in your life while you have been single?

*5.* Are your affairs in order? Are you financially stable? Do you have a bunch of junk in your house that needs to be thrown away or donated to charity? In other words, are you prepared in practical ways for a major life change? If not, how will you get prepared?

## *Learn Your Lines*

*He who finds a wife finds a good thing,*
*and obtains favor from the Lord.*
**Proverbs 18:22**

*Who can find a virtuous wife?*
*For her worth is far above rubies.*
**Proverbs 31:10, 11**

# COMING SOON

*L*eading lady, what freedom you have as you look at your life on your own and gaze upon your future! But perhaps the busy-ness and the responsibilities you carry may have dampened some of your dreams and caused you to grow weary. Now is the time to celebrate who you are, and to rejoice in all the possibilities that lie ahead. It is time to blow the dust off the dreams on the shelves of your heart. Perhaps years of singleness have snuffed out your dreams of marriage and children.

It is time to dream of love again! Let your heart take you back to your dreams for a few moments, whatever those dreams are for you as a single woman, and let your pen record them.

_____

_____

_____

_____

_____

_____

_____

_____

_____

_____

# ACTION!

$\mathcal{B}$ased on what you have learned in this chapter, what are three concise, measurable, attainable goals you will set for yourself as a single woman? Be sure to include a schedule and target date for reaching each goal and a reward for accomplishing it.

*1.* Goal:
Schedule and target completion date:
Reward:

*2.* Goal:
Schedule and target completion date:
Reward:

*3.* Goal:
Schedule and target completion date:
Reward:

# 4
# The Lady and Her Lover

## Introducing

o, you find yourself with a ring on your finger! Maybe you have worn that ring for forty years, or maybe it still has its showroom sparkle. Regardless, I am of the opinion that the changing nature of life leaves room for improvement in all relationships, whether they are in their infancy or whether they have a history that stretches over a long period of time.

When I write about your lover, I am referring to the man with whom you share your life within the bond of marriage, the God-given partner to whom you are legally wed and with whom you are following God's divine plan. If there is such a man in your life, I think you will find the information in this chapter helpful as the two of you waltz across life's stage together. You can read more of my teaching and insights on marriage in two of my books: *The Lady, Her Lover, and Her Lord* and *God's Leading Lady*.

# The Main Event

## Act 1: The Magnificent Marriage

Your marriage is the second most important relationship in your life. (Your relationship with the Lord, of course, is primary). The sacred blend of your life with your husband's produces a beautiful symphony that inspires everyone who hears it and even pleases heaven with its glorious sound. That's what I want for your life, and that's what you can have as you take your place as a leading lady, alongside God's chosen leading man.

One of the most important aspects of marriage I can focus on in this chapter is trust, and if I could only encourage you to be one thing to your husband, it would be for you to be a woman he can truly trust. Would you read in the Bible verses below and pay particular attention to the fact that the first quality of a woman that is mentioned in this famous passage of scripture is that "the heart of her husband safely trusts her?"

*Who can find a virtuous wife?*
*For her worth is far above rubies.*
*The heart of her husband safely trusts her;*
*So he will have no lack of gain.*
*She does him good and not evil all the days of her life.*
**Proverbs 31:10–12**

Throughout my years in ministry, I have counseled a multitude of men and can assure you that this issue of trust is critically important to men when they think about their relationships with women. Sharing the matters of the heart comes more easily to women than to men, so would you allow me now to share with you from a man's heart and a man's perspective? There are many areas in which your man needs to be able to trust you, but for our purposes here, let's concentrate on a few of the most important.

You probably know already, but I will remind you, that women are a mystery to men. We are intrigued by you, but our fascination does nothing to help us understand you. Therefore, it is crucial that we are able to trust your motives. We may not understand what you do or say, but if we can trust that you are speaking or acting with noble, selfless intentions, we can relax. If we know your motives are pure and that you really do have our best interest at heart, then we are at ease and can rest in your love.

Second, we must be able to trust you sexually. Your man needs to be convinced that he is the center of your sexual universe (and he should be!) and that you would not even think of allowing your eye to wander. Furthermore, he needs to be able to trust your responses to him and to know that you will be honest about your intimate moments together. He does not want you to react for his entertainment; he wants to know that he genuinely pleases you. Beyond that, he needs to know that what takes place in your bedroom stays behind closed doors. The quickest way on earth to infuriate your man is for his lovemaking skills to become the topic of conversation at the next girl's night out. Marriage is an intimate relationship, so guard the trust of your sexual intimacy diligently!

> *A recent survey concluded that: 80% of the relationships in which couples were living together without marriage vows end in separation. 60% of those who are married by a justice of the peace are divorced later. 40% of those who are married in churches eventually divorce. And those who read their Bibles together daily divorce at the rate of 1 out of 1,050!*[1]

Your man must also trust you to be consistent. He does better when he can trust that hormones will not turn you into a woman he's never met before, that you will not revisit a matter that the two of you have already resolved and throw some new twist into the conversation, that emotions will not cause your personality to change, and that you will not break down in tears or shut down in anger toward him. He needs you to be steady and stable and dependable.

Lady, when a man trusts you enough to share his heart with you, he also needs to trust you to keep his secrets and not to use his openness against him. Believe it or not, a man's feelings are precious and he wants to be able to trust you to protect them as much as he does.

You can help establish trust in your relationship by simply listening when he is willing to share. Listen without judging, without analyzing, and without jumping to conclusions. Chances are that he is able to come up with his own solution (men are just like that), but that he just needs a safe place to unload.

*Listen without judging, without analyzing, and without jumping to conclusions.*

Finally, he needs to be able to trust you not to compete with him. This is true professionally, socially and in parenting situations—just to name a few. When competition enters a marriage, no one emerges victorious. True love builds up the other person and puts his interests ahead of your own. If he can trust you not to be his rival, he will trust you more as his wife.

As I wrote to you earlier, these thoughts alone are not enough to build an entire relationship, but they are good foundation stones. With a solid base of trust underneath your interaction with your man, you will be on your way to a truly magnificent marriage.

# *You're On*

*1.* What do you admire, appreciate, or treasure most about your man? In what ways do you compliment each other?

*2.* What commitments to excellence do you and your husband share?

*3.* What does your man need most from you? I am not asking you what you think he needs or what you wish he would need. I am asking you what he really needs.

*4.* Are you a safe haven for the man you love? In what areas do you need to be more understanding? Do you keep his secrets or do you need to be more confidential?

# *Learn Your Lines*

So God created man in His own image; in the image of God
He created him; male and female He created them.

**Genesis 1:27**

Then the rib which the Lord God had taken from man
He made into a woman, and He brought her to the man.

**Genesis 2:22**

Nevertheless, let each one of you [men] in particular so love his own
wife as himself, and let the wife see that she respects her husband.

**Ephesians 5:33**

And be kind to one another, tenderhearted, forgiving one another,
even as God in Christ forgave you.

**Ephesians 4:32**

Let the husband render to his wife the affection due her;
and likewise also the wife to her husband.

**1 Corinthians 7:3**

## *Act 2: Twelve Truths About Men*

*1.* He doesn't understand you either.

*2.* He does not realize that you do not really want answers when you ask questions and that you do not really want a solution when you mention a problem.

*3.* When he feels vulnerable or insecure, he will crawl into a shell like a turtle. He wants you to feel safe and secure and does not like to reveal his own insecurities.

*4.* He would appreciate not having to figure out what's wrong. Explain yourself and be direct.

*5.* He may seem as though he doesn't want to talk, but he does want you to listen.

*6.* He probably says, "I love you" in an entirely different language than you do.

*7.* He needs to hear you tell him how much you admire and respect him. Words of affirmation make him feel ten feet tall.

*8.* He does not know what to do with your emotional outbursts.

*9.* He is visual. He will appreciate your efforts to look good for him.

*10.* He wants to be wanted. He needs to be needed (and he needs you, too).

*11.* He does not want to answer as many questions as you want to ask. This causes him to feel overexposed.

*12.* He will always return to the one with whom his heart is safe.

> *He needs to hear you tell him how much you admire and respect him. Words of affirmation make him feel ten feet tall.*

# *You're On*

*1.* Do you know yourself well enough to explain to a man what's bugging you and why, or do you just get so emotional that you cannot even articulate the problem? If you are prone to outbursts you can't explain, how can you begin to help yourself understand you so that you can communicate better with your man?

> *He will always return to the one with whom his heart is safe.*

*2.* How can you process your issues better internally so that your man does not feel as though he is standing in court being questioned when you begin to tell him what's going on? What is the most effective way for you to share your life as you talk to him?

*3.* If you already know your man, how does he say, "I love you,"? If not, when you meet someone, watch to see how he expresses love. Can his expression meet your needs? If not, how can you help him in an affirming way?

## *Learn Your Lines*

*Love suffers long and is kind; love does not envy;*
*love does not parade itself, is not puffed up; does not behave rudely,*
*does not seek its own, is not provoked, thinks no evil.*
**1 Corinthians 13: 4, 5**

*And above all things have fervent love for one another,*
*for "love will cover a multitude of sins."*
**1 Peter 4:8**

### *Act 3: When the Lights Go Down*

If you have been married for any length of time, you know what to do when you and your man are alone behind the bedroom door. You know the mechanics and you know the rhythm of your sex life with your man. I don't need to instruct you in those areas or to explain anything to you. But I do want to make sure you understand one thing that is very important to your man: he needs feedback. Whether your sex life is red-hot or about to fizzle out, feedback from you will help your man more than you can imagine.

Think about it. When you cook a delicious meal—and you feel good about your performance with spatulas and mixing bowls and the oven—you want to hear him tell you that you prepared the best meal in the entire universe. You want him to tell you that those chefs on television could not have done it any better. You want to hear how the subtle flavors blended together and how much he could sense your love because of the fabulous meal you prepared. Am I right? Maybe you don't get that kind of feedback, but am I correct that you would like to?

What's true for you in the kitchen is true for your man in the bedroom. Here are five specific kinds of feedback he needs.

*1.* First, he needs to know that your feedback is for his ears alone. It is vital to his self-esteem.

*2.* He needs to know when he pleases you and when he does not. Affirm him when he does and tell him gently when he does not.

*3.* He needs honest responses. If you do not tell him the truth, he will feel inadequate and manipulated.

*4.* He would appreciate feedback outside the bedroom. You can let him know how much you appreciate him when the lights are low with a smile or a wink. You can do this gracefully and discreetly. He will get the message.

*5.* He would like your feedback at times by hearing you request him, not by your always waiting for him to make amorous advances toward you. He knows you've tasted something good and are hungry for more if you ask.

## *You're On*

*1.* Are you happy with your sex life? How would you like to see it improve?

*2.* Do you give your husband the kinds of feedback described?

*3.* What changes will you make in order to communicate your responses to your husband in regard to your sex life?

# *Learn Your Lines*

And they were both naked, the man and his wife,
and were not ashamed.

**Genesis 2:25**

Marriage is honorable among all, and the bed undefiled;
but fornicators and adulterers God will judge.

**Hebrews 13:4**

His mouth is most sweet, yes, he is altogether lovely.
This is my beloved, and this is my friend.

**Song of Solomon 5:16**

The wife does not have authority over her own body, but the husband
does. And likewise the husband does not have authority over his own
body, but the wife does. Do not deprive one another except with consent
for a time, that you may give yourselves to fasting and prayer;
and come together again so that Satan does not tempt you
because of your lack of self-control.

**1 Corinthians 7:4, 5**

# COMING SOON

*L*ady, there is a good chance that you have dreamed about your marriage since you were a little girl. Most little girls do. But there is also a chance that your marriage has not been a dream fulfilled. I must tell you that change is possible. I must tell you that there is power in true love—that the most painful marriage can be healed and that even the deadest relationship can be revived. Would you ask your heart to dream again? Now that the little girl you once were has become the woman you are, now that the marriage you dreamed of has become the relationship you have—what do you hope for? What do you want to see for yourself and the man you love? Even if your marriage is magnificent, there is always room for improvement, there is always more to hope for!

_____

_____

_____

_____

_____

_____

_____

_____

# ACTION!

*B*ased on what you have learned in this chapter, what are three concise, measurable, attainable goals you will set for yourself in your relationship with the man you love? Be sure to include a schedule and target date for reaching each goal and a reward for accomplishing it.

*1.* Goal:
  Schedule and target completion date:
  Reward:

*2.* Goal:
  Schedule and target completion date:
  Reward:

*3.* Goal:
  Schedule and target completion date:
  Reward:

# 5

# *The Lady Keeps Her Balance*

### *Introducing*

One of the most important ingredients in a truly successful life is balance—giving every element of life its proper weight and priority as you live day by day. Leading ladies need to be aware that one of the great temptations of success is to overwork or over commit in the areas of your expertise. For instance, when you are enjoying seasons of professional achievement or recognition, you may be tempted to devote too much time and energy to your career. The problem is that in the midst of working so hard, you may inadvertently neglect your family or even your own personal needs. There are only so many hours in every day, and in order to maximize them and to be a good steward over everything God has given you, you will need to endeavor to maintain balance in all areas of your life.

# *The Main Event*

## *Act 1: Oh, What Lovely Hats You Have!*

If you are like most leading ladies, you have too many hats and your head is not big enough to accommodate all of them at the same time! You have your Person hat, perhaps your Wife hat, maybe a Mother hat, probably a Work hat, your Daughter hat, and your Friend hat. And no doubt you have a closet full of other hats as well.

Through years of ministry, I have observed many things about people, and one is that they rarely need to be encouraged to work harder or longer or to be more driven on the job. This is especially true for leading ladies. I rarely preach the funeral of someone whose family says to me, "Well, Bishop, we just wish she had worked more. We really wish she had spent less time with us and made fewer sacrifices." I would be shocked to hear a family express such sentiments!

No, what I often have to do is remind people to stop along life's path and smell its roses. Life's roses include family and friends; special times together; time just for you; a balanced work life; the joy of seeing your children succeed; being there to kiss a skinned knee or to watching a butterfly emerge from its cocoon; asking your parents about their childhood hopes and dreams, their fears and regrets, the things that have made their lives memorable; sharing your life with someone else; stopping for a cup of coffee with a friend. These are the kinds of things that seem to get pushed aside as our responsibilities increase with a promotion, marriage, children, or with caring for someone elderly or infirm.

> *I want you to be a success in every area of your life. That will require you to establish your priorities so you can make time for the people and things most important to you.*

I challenge you to look at your hats. Perhaps you are wearing them well, changing them quickly and generally succeeding when it comes to all the roles you must play. Then again, perhaps they are littering the floor of the closet of your life and you have no energy to put any of them on again. If that is the case, chances are there is a bouquet of dead roses buried beneath all those hats. Something has to give, lady. I want you to be a success in every area of your life. That will require you to establish your priorities so you can make time for the people and things most important to you. So think about the questions below, and then move on to Acts 2 and 3 of this chapter, where you will learn how to improve your balance in life and how to set boundaries that will help you enforce your priorities.

## *You're On*

*1.* Does your husband "feel the love," or have you let the pressing demands of your life crowd him out? What can you do to let him know how special he is to you?

*2.* Are you satisfied with the amount and the quality of the time you spend with your family? What is it you really long to plant and nurture in your children? Are you doing this?

*3.* In your heart, do you really honor your father and your mother? How can you express honor toward your parents in practical, every-day ways?

*4.* Are you being a good friend? To whom do you owe a phone call or lunch? How are you going to better tend to your friendships in the days to come?

*5.* If you are having trouble wearing all your hats, you must start by prioritizing your life. Take a moment now to list the roles you play and then rank them in order of their importance to you. Then, *voila*! There are your priorities!

# Learn Your Lines

*Listen to your father who begot you,*
*and do not despise your mother when she is old.*
**Proverbs 23:22**

*. . . do not provoke your children to wrath, but bring them up*
*in the training and admonition of the Lord.*
**Ephesians 6:2**

*A man who has friends must himself be friendly . . .*
**Proverbs 18:22a**

## Act 2: Staying Steady

Have you ever watched the women's gymnastics competition during the Olympic games? A teenage girl makes her routines look absolutely effortless as she flips and glides and twirls up and down the length of a balance beam as though it is a mile wide. But if you gaze upon her face, you will see the concentration in her eyes; you will see her purse her lips as she focuses, focuses, focuses; you will see the fierce intensity of a seasoned competitor.

As she springs into action, you witness the results of years of practice and discipline, and the fruit of everything she's learned by falling off that beam more times than she can count. No matter how difficult her program, she will only be awarded a high score if she stays on the beam, if she keeps her balance, and stays steady. No matter how complicated her moves may be, if she tumbles to the floor instead of landing on the beam, she is not likely to win a medal.

*There are thousands of areas of our life, and each one of them has to be brought into balance and then kept that way through regular maintenance and proper care.*[1]

Like the gymnast, a leading lady must learn to balance all the demands of life. And a true leading lady will not only be able to walk the balance beam of her daily duties, she will be able to glide gracefully through her obligations and to flip into some things that are fun for her. She will twirl with confidence, knowing that she has mastered the art of balance so she can keep her footing in any situation. She knows the only way she can be complete is to be balanced. She will veer neither to the right nor to the left.

*The delicate art of balance is only possible as you keep your gaze fixed on The Lord and allow His word to keep you steady.*

Just as the gymnast must practice, practice, practice in order to be able to give a winning performance, you may also have to experiment with different approaches and strategies for balancing your life. You will not only need to learn to balance your time, you will also have to balance the many roles you play. The delicate art of balance is only possible as you keep your gaze fixed on the Lord and allow His Word to keep you steady. I don't think it can be done without prayer or without seeking Him for creative ways to handle the many situations you are dealing with. But He is ultimately creative, and I have every confidence that, as you commune with Him regarding this matter, He will not only teach you to walk the balance beam, but to do so with grace—and maybe even with a few breathtaking flips and turns!

# You're On

*1.* In what areas of your life have you fallen off the beam completely?

*2.* In what areas do you feel yourself slipping?

*3.* How are you going to get back on the beam where you have fallen off?

*4.* How are you going to adjust your life so that you are balanced in the areas where you are slipping? (Hint: you may have to give up some things and enforce stricter priorities.)

*A prayerful look at your friendships will determine whether you need to begin building boundaries with some of your friends. By setting boundaries, you may save some important ones.*[2]

**5.** When a person is falling to the left, she will often lean too far to the right in order to regain her balance. But if she stays that way, she will simply fall off the other side. What are you going to do in order to keep yourself steady and maintain your balance in your busy life?

## *Learn Your Lines*

*To everything there is a season, a time for every purpose under heaven.*

**Ecclesiastes 3:1**

*Ponder the path of your feet, and let all your ways be established.*

**Proverbs 4:26**

*Test all things; hold fast what is good.*

**2 Thessalonians 5:21**

### *Act 3: Coloring Within the Lines*

Do you remember, as a little girl, when you first learned to color? In the beginning, parents and teachers were so delighted by your ability to hold a crayon in your little fingers that they allowed you to scribble all over large, blank sheets of paper. As you gained better command of the crayon, however, someone probably gave you a coloring book in order to teach you how to control the crayon by staying within the lines.

Life is like that coloring book. Everything has boundaries, and the big picture is much prettier when we stay inside the lines.

Boundaries must be established one the job, with your family and friends, in your relationships with men, and in every other significant area of your life.

Just as you were solely in charge of coloring within the lines so many years ago, now you alone are responsible for maintaining the boundaries of your life. As long as you are a leading lady, there will be people who want to follow and people who place demands on you. Because you are not anyone's life source, the best way to handle the never-ending stream of needs is to know when to say "Enough" and then be able to graciously direct them to the God who never runs out.

## *You're On*

*1.* Think specifically about your job. Have you set appropriate boundaries on the job, or are you a person about whom others say, "Oh, get so-and-so to work late. She's single. She has nothing else to do!" How can you identify and implement the proper boundaries?

> *Boundary setting is a large part of maturing. We can't really love until we have boundaries—otherwise we love out of compliance or guilt.*[3]

*2.* Think about your relationship with your family. Are proper boundaries in place? How can you put the right boundaries in place?

*3.* What about your relationships with men? Have you established godly boundaries and communicated them clearly? How can you start enforcing boundaries immediately?

*4.* In what other areas of your life do you need to build boundaries? How will you do that?

## *Learn Your Lines*

*The lines have fallen to me in pleasant places; yes,*
*I have a good inheritance.*

**Psalm 16:6**

*Whoever has no rule over his own spirit*
*is like a city broken down, without walls.*

**Proverbs 25:28**

*Rejoice always, pray without ceasing, in everything give thanks;*
*for this is the will of God in Christ Jesus for you.*

**1 Thessalonians 5:16–18**

# COMING SOON

*P*erhaps you have extended yourself to the point that you have no time or energy left to invest in the precious person you are. Put on paper what you will do in the very near future to put appropriate boundaries in place. Perhaps the pressures of a career have quenched your creativity. Right now, write down the creative things you'd like to do—and need to do! Write down your idea of a perfect play day, a day with no deadlines or demands. Or write down what you would like to do with your best friend (and then schedule it).

_____

_____

_____

_____

_____

_____

_____

_____

_____

_____

# ACTION!

*B*ased on what you have learned in this chapter, what are three concise, measurable, attainable goals you will set for yourself in the areas of balance and boundaries? Be sure to include a schedule and target date for reaching each goal and a reward for accomplishing it.

*1.* Goal:
Schedule and target completion date:
Reward:

*2.* Goal:
Schedule and target completion date:
Reward:

*3.* Goal:
Schedule and target completion date:
Reward:

# 6

# The Lady and Her Legacy

## Introducing

There will come a day—perhaps it is already here—when you have triumphed over the years in the wonderful way that only *you* can. Your head is crowned with white and your face is graced with the lines that could be a map of your lifelong journey of ups and downs, victories and defeats, smiles and tears. Whatever your life has held, it has been *your* life and it has taught you unique lessons and it is the content of the legacy you will leave to your co-workers once you retire, to your community once you are no longer able to be active, and to your friends and family once you have moved out of their lives and into the presence of God. Lady, you have so much to give, so much to share, and if you are going to keep leading long after you have stepped out of the spotlight, you will need to leave behind more than your estate; you will need to leave behind the legacy of your soul.

# The Main Event

## Act 1: The Privilege of the Latter Years

I have a term I like to use when describing the kind of serene and gracious older woman who has made peace with her past, embraced her present, and looks forward to every dawning day with gratitude. I call her "the winter woman." It is the winter women alone who greet life with the gift of wisdom they could only have purchased by the nitty-gritty experiences that come with year after year of authentic living. Yes, it is the winter women who so often hold life's treasures, for they have lived long enough to have a perspective the young cannot.

And yet, our modern culture fights aging with a fury. We fail to draw from the wells of experience that lie deep within those whose hair is gray, whose faces are wrinkled, and whose teeth have fallen out. For the leading lady, it is important to look and feel young for as long as you want, but in doing so, remember to age gracefully. Recognize that the years take their toll on everyone and the unique privilege of winter days is a treasure chest of lessons and wisdom that are desperately needed by those around you.

> *Recognize that the years take their toll on everyone and that the unique privilege of winter days is a treasure chest of lessons and wisdom that are desperately needed by those around you.*[1]

## *You're On*

*1.* What is the greatest lesson or truth you know? (Of course, you can list more than one.)

*God never extends days beyond purpose.*[2]

*2.* What privileges or opportunities can you enjoy in your latter years that you could not previously enjoy?

*3.* Is there a Bible verse or a quotation that has guided your life? If so, what is it? If not, maybe you would like to choose one or write your own now.

*4.* What are you looking forward to?

## *Learn Your Lines*

*Those who are planted in the house of the Lord shall flourish
in the courts of our God. They shall still bear fruit in old age;
they shall be fresh and flourishing.*

**Psalm 92:13, 14**

*Even to your old age, I am He, and even to gray hairs I will carry you!
I have made, and I will bear; even I will carry, and I will deliver you.*

**Isaiah 46:2**

*Leave
something
behind that points
to who you
were.*[3]

## Act 2: More Influential than Ever

If you have found yourself with more birthdays behind you than in front of you, consider this: just because you may not move as quickly as you once did does not mean there are no contributions left for you to make to the world in which you live. There is something you can do regardless of how agile or infirm you are. You may find yourself with more time on your hands than you have had in the past—and that's what puts you in position to be more influential now than ever. It may sound simple, but the secret of this enormous influence is found in a four-letter word: p-r-a-y.

You see, when you pray for the people you love, your influence is not earthly and fleeting; it is spiritual and infinite. As you beseech almighty God to intervene in the lives of your loved ones, you can move heaven and earth with your heartfelt cries. As you pray, you are sowing eternal seed into the destinies of those for whom you intercede—and that is the most life-changing, effective influence of all.

In addition to your conversations with God, I encourage you to sit and talk with your children, your grandchildren, people you have mentored, and others who would like to mine the gold inside of you. Share freely, for your wisdom multiplies as you give it away.

You see, there is something that happens when you pray for people. You begin to care more and more—even if you did not think it was possible to care any more deeply. And then, when you are with those people, they can sense the depth of interest you have in their lives. Then they want to reach into your soul and learn what you know. They want to be for others the kind of friend or relative you are to them. And the cycle of influence continues . . .

> *You are never too old to give birth to your dreams. The story ain't over till it's over.*[4]

## *You're On*

*1.* Over whom do you hold the most influence right now, whether that influence is as direct as having that person living under your roof, or whether you rarely see that person and exert your influence through prayer?

*When you pray for the people you love, your influence is not earthly and fleeting; it is spiritual and infinite.*

*2.* In what areas of influence do you need to be more intentional?

*3.* How can you transfer the lessons you have learned to those who come after you—through art, through writing them down, through photographs? What will you do to preserve your legacy and your influence?

*4.* How would you like to be remembered?

## *Learn Your Lines*

*Let my prayer be set before You as incense,*
*the lifting of my hands as the evening sacrifice.*

**Psalm 141:2**

*Wisdom is with aged men, and with length of days, understanding.*

**Job 12:12**

*For this is God, our God forever and ever;*
*and He will be our guide even to death.*

**Psalm 48:14**

*As you pray, you are sowing eternal seed into the destinies of those for whom you intercede — and that is the most life-changing, effective influence of all.*

# COMING SOON

Whether you are in the springtime, the autumn, or the winter of your life, you're bound to think of growing older and I'm sure you may ask yourself at times, "Is it worth it?" I don't want to presume that I know what you mean when you ask that question, but is it possible that what you really want is the assurance that everything you have done and are doing with your life will matter? I believe you want to reach the end of your days with the conviction that you really made a difference, not necessarily to corporate budgets or to professional projects most people have forgotten, but a rich and long-term investment in the lives of those you love. As you think about what's ahead for you, allow yourself to dream beyond your own mortality. What would you like your life to speak once your lips are forever still? What is your legacy?

_____

_____

_____

_____

_____

_____

_____

# ACTION!

*B*ased on what you have learned in this chapter, what are three concise, measurable, attainable goals you will set for your own latter years or in your relationships with older women in your life? Be sure to include a schedule and target date for reaching each goal and a reward for accomplishing it.

*1.* Goal:
Schedule and target completion date:
Reward:

*2.* Goal:
Schedule and target completion date:
Reward:

*3.* Goal:
Schedule and target completion date:
Reward:

# 7

# The Lady at Work

## Introducing

any, many women are employed these days. Some are self-employed; some work for a company or ministry; others own or run these companies or ministries. Some women are employed because they want to be, and others because they have to be. We spend a lot of time working, and my desire is that you would be as fulfilled as possible on the job, that you would be an excellent employee or boss who would scale the heights of your chosen profession and plant your flag on its summit!

## The Main Event

### Act 1: A Job to Do

If you are looking for a job, you need to know why. That may sound strange, but when it comes to work, a lot of women fail to allow their passions and talents to impact their job decisions as much as they probably should. And so, I beg you to really understand why you are looking for a job. Your answer may be as simple as the fact that your husband has left you and you are forced to find employment, or it may be that you have finally decided to pursue your dream and forget about spending your days behind a desk when what you really want to do is arrange flowers. Then again, you may want to stay in your field, but you are tired of bumping your head on the glass ceiling imposed by race or gender and you need to find an employer who will recognize and reward your intelligence and your diligence.

It is so important for you to do something you love and something that fills your life with purpose. Once you know why you are job hunting, you will know better what kinds of jobs to look for. True, you may need to take a job that is not your dream job so you can pay your bills, but determine to let that be a temporary situation. Your life is too short for you to be miserable forty hours a week.

As you begin to investigate possible places of employment, ask friends about the places where they work or do business; search the want ads; visit websites such as www.monster.com. Technology can really be a friend to you in the job search because so many employers post job openings on their websites. Once you get serious about where you'd like to apply, consider consulting the Better Business Bureau to see if any complaints have been lodged against that company. This can save you a lot of heartache. Do as much research as you can. Even paying attention to the frequency of one company's want ads could help you—if they regularly advertise for the same position, there is probably a reason that job does not stay filled. On the other hand, if you keep your eyes and ears open, good places to work will often surface in local newspapers or magazines or by word-of-mouth.

Once you have decided what you would like to do, you may need to have an interview or a series of interviews with the companies you contact. Interviewing for a position at a bank or a law firm will have a different feel than interviewing at a design firm or a music company. Regardless of where you go,

*It is so important that you do something you love and something that fills your life with purpose.*

here are several good, all-purpose tips to remember when interviewing for a job.

◆ Be on time, or a few minutes early. Though a potential employer may keep you waiting, you must not keep that person waiting. Tardiness never makes a good first impression.

◆ Many businesses have switched from a coat-and-tie/hose-and-heels dress code to what we call "business casual." It is awkward to be overdressed for an interview, so inquire about the dress code when you speak with the person who arranges your interview.

◆ Based on the dress code where you are going, dress appropriately. Make sure your shoes are clean and polished, that your handbag is well-kept, and that your pantyhose (if you need to wear them) are free from runs.

◆ Answer questions thoroughly, but do not get "diarrhea of the mouth" and keep talking after you have responded appropriately.

◆ Do not speak negatively about a former employer. Find a way to cast your job search in a positive light—even if you have to think awfully hard in order to do so.

◆ Never underestimate yourself, but do be honest about your skills and experience.

◆ Be sensitive to the time you have been allotted.

◆ As you are leaving, thank the person or people who interview you. Write a thank-you note within one week.

> *If you keep your eyes and ears open, good places to work will often surface in local newspapers or magazines or by word-of-mouth.*

## *You're On*

*1.* What is your favorite thing to do? Can you find a way to get paid for doing it?

*2.* Do you have everything you need in order to make a good impression during an interview? If not, what do you need to do or have? How will you do this?

*3.* Have you prayerfully considered all of your job options? Are you willing to wait for God's best in the area of employment? If you must work immediately, are you willing to take an intermediate step on the way to your dream job?

## *Learn Your Lines*

*For each one shall bear his own load.*
**Galatians 6:5**

*In all labor, there is profit, but idle chatter leads only to poverty.*
**Proverbs 14:23**

*If anyone will not work, neither shall he eat.*
**2 Thessalonians 3:10b**

### *Act 2: Doing It Right*

Once you have a job, you want to make sure you do it right. The first day on the job is as unnerving for some people as the first day of school, but it is easier to have a strong beginning than to overcome a false start. Once you've gotten established, maintain your good practices. Standards and expectations vary from one job to another, but I can give you at least four suggestions—some you may not find in other materials that deal with employment—that will apply to every situation.

*Be grateful.* Even if your job is not what you imagine as the perfect job for you, you applied for the job for a reason. You were hired for a reason. This job will be a means of God's provision for you for as long as you have it.

*Listen.* Even if you have been hired as the boss, chances are that the people who have been there longer than you can share some valuable insight on the company or ministry. Solicit input from various sources so you do not get a lopsided report; and then let history be one of your teachers.

*Pray.* Oh, how I believe that God wants to move mightily in the marketplace—in the corporations, the courts, the hospitals, and the schools—the technology sector of our nation! I believe He wants to make His glory known in government, the media, and the entertainment world. Is it possible, leading lady, that you are His appointed ambassador to your sphere of influence through your job? Believe that it just may be. And pray as if you are the only pray-er there!

*Serve, even if you are the leader.* Serve, *especially* if you are the leader. Ask God to guide you as you serve others. I want to specifically encourage you to ask Him to lead you and then to hear and obey what He says. He may cast you in the role of a servant, even though you are a leader, by asking you to do something like refill the copy machine or the coffee pot—even though those tasks are not your job. He may ask you to give someone a ride home when their car is in the shop. Ask God for opportunities to serve, regardless of your position on the corporate ladder—and then watch, for they will come.

*Practice honor toward your superiors.* You do not have to like your boss or bosses, but it is crucial that you respect their positions of authority over you and that you honor them as leaders. That kind of humility not only makes people wonder what you are made of, it also helps bring peace and order in the workplace as others observe your attitude and behavior. Furthermore, it opens doors for greater things down the road.

In addition, it is important that the excellence in your life spill over into your work.

◆ Be on time for your job.

◆ Keep your workspace neat and clean.

◆ Perform your duties with excellence.

◆ Be respectful of others.

◆ Don't make promises you can't keep.

◆ Do not cheat the clock.

# *You're On*

*1.* All right sister, it's time to get honest. Are you on time for work? Do you work all the hours you are supposed to? Do you keep your workspace neat and business affairs organized? Answer yes or no in the space below. If you answer no to either question, write also what you will do in order to change your ways.

*The first day on the job is as unnerving for some people as the first day of school, but it is easier to have a strong beginning than to overcome a false start.*

*2.* Do you pray for and honor those who are in authority over you because of their leadership positions—even if those people are difficult to work for?

*3.* The apostle Paul wrote in Titus 3:1, 2: "Remind them to be subject to rulers and authorities, to obey, to be ready for every good work, to speak evil of no one, to be peaceable, gentle, showing all humility to all [people]." Does this describe your attitude and your behavior in the workplace? If not, what adjustments do you need to make in order to line up your life with the Word?

# *Learn Your Lines*

*Whatever your hand finds to do, do it with your might . . .*
**Ecclesiastes 9:10a**

*And whatever you do, in word or deed, do all in the name of the Lord Jesus, giving thanks to God the Father through Him.*
**Colossians 3:17**

*Remind them to be subject to rulers and authorities, to obey, to be ready for every good work, to speak evil of no one, to be peaceable, gentle, showing humility to all men.*
**Titus 3:1, 2**

## *Act 3: Going To the Next Level*

God's desire is to prosper you and to fill your life with increase. He has put within you the desire to grow, to excel, and to be promoted into places of greater authority and/or influence. He wants you operating at maximum capacity and He has a great plan in place for your advancement! I believe He has you on the path of greatness and when that is the case, something happens. That job you were once excited about begins to drive you nuts. You stop feeling challenged in the good way, but challenged because it has become too restrictive. You begin to feel like a large bird in a small cage.

So what's a woman to do when she finds her feathers sticking out of the cage? She is to seek, trust, and walk in the wisdom of her heavenly Father.

The Bible says, "The steps of a good man are ordered by the Lord" (Proverbs 37:23)—and that's equally true for a good woman! I want to assure you that His plan for you is infinitely wise and He has nothing but your best interest in mind. You must remember this when you are telling Him you will explode if you have to spend one more day sitting in that cubicle, or standing at that cash register, or arguing before that particular judge.

Job transition, especially when it will end in a place of great destiny, reminds me of transition during the physical birthing process. A woman will think she absolutely cannot stand it any more; she will think thoughts that are not becoming to a lady of her quality; she will say things that would shock a sailor's ears! The pressure is so intense that she only wants one thing: to be put out of her misery. But there is only one way out, and that is to push—at the right time—until the baby is born. The same is true for you as you move to the next level in your career. If you have chosen your job carefully and at the direction of the Holy Spirit, then it is part of your destiny training. When it is time for promotion, you must know when to push through that frustration and when to wisely keep your mouth shut and just do what you are supposed to do. You will have to know when to push through genuine obstacles and when to accept delays as part of God's timing. Keep praying, keep worshiping, keep living by the Word, and you will see that God's promotion is perfect for you!

## *You're On*

*1.* After you have prayed and sought God concerning your career path, what do you think He would have you do now or in the near future in order to position yourself to move into the next place He has for you?

*2.* Have you honestly evaluated your potential for promotion where you are currently employed? If there is a legitimate "glass ceiling" in place, are you prepared to change companies? If you need to do that, where will you look?

*3.* How can you apply the wisdom of God to your work situation, especially as it relates to your future?

# *Learn Your Lines*

*Then this Daniel distinguished himself above the governors and satraps, because an excellent spirit was in him; and the king gave thought to setting him over the whole realm.*

**Daniel 6:3**

*So David went out wherever Saul sent him, and behaved wisely. And Saul set him over the men of war, and he was accepted in the sight of all the people and also in the sight of Saul's servants.*

**1 Samuel 18:5**

*He who is faithful in what is least is also faithful in much . . .*

**Luke 16:10**

*If the ax is dull, and one does not sharpen the edge, then he must use more strength; but wisdom brings success.*

**Ecclesiastes 10:10**

# COMING SOON

*O*ne way or another, all leading ladies have to make a living. Occasionally, a generous husband prefers to provide for his lady, but often, leading ladies want or need to exercise their gifts and talents in some sort of employment situation. I ask you, are you happy in your work? Are you contributing to society the way you want to, and are you fulfilling what you believe to be God's best plan for your life? Whether now is the time for you to get a job, quit a job, start your own business, or climb the corporate ladder, you spend many hours investing yourself in your work. So won't you take a few moments right now to think and dream about what you really need and want to be doing?

_____

_____

_____

_____

_____

_____

_____

_____

_____

_____

# ACTION!

$\mathcal{B}$ased on what you have learned in this chapter, what are three concise, measurable, attainable goals you will set for yourself as you seek or maintain, and as you flourish in your workplace? Be sure to include a schedule and target date for reaching each goal and a reward for accomplishing it.

1. Goal:
   Schedule and target completion date:
   Reward:

2. Goal:
   Schedule and target completion date:
   Reward:

3. Goal:
   Schedule and target completion date:
   Reward:

# 8

# The Lady in Charge

## Introducing

lot of leaders are bosses, but a lot of bosses are not leaders. I'll tell you a secret: leadership requires brains and courage and vision, but it cannot live long if it is only fed by those things. The foundation of true, godly leadership is the leader's ability to relate well. In order to lead in such a way that God's purposes can be fulfilled in the leader, the people she leads and the organization she leads, she needs to have a solid relationship with Him and the ability to relate well to others. All leaders need people who are willing and eager to serve their vision—and the only way to raise up loyal, happy employees is to be able to relate to them. (If all people ever hear is a bossy voice ordering them from one task to the next, they will be miserable and will soon be gone!) Furthermore, the leader must relate to the various people and entities outside her own responsibilities if she is going to be respected in her industry and in her community, even if her community covers the globe.

I salute you, woman in charge. I say to you, lead on! Take your place in leadership, keep developing as a leader, and handle well the success that comes your way!

# The Main Event

## Act 1: Taking Your Place

Whatever your sphere of influence or expertise, there comes that appointed moment when the spotlight turns toward you. You land the starring role; you finish the project; you get the promotion; you win the award. And you are a leader. Other people look up to you; they value your insight and your perspective; they seek your counsel; they act on your recommendations. You have the power to influence them, which is the essence of leadership.

Some women are like racehorses who have been pushing against the starting gate for so long that when they are released into leadership, they meet the challenge with all the power of a thoroughbred thundering down the track. Other women are more reluctant leaders, accepting the call to lead, but wary of leadership's responsibilities and hesitant concerning their own abilities. To both kinds of women, I have the same advice: take your place.

To the thoroughbred, take your place as you fan the flames of that natural confidence and strength, but take it wisely. You have already earned respect—your leadership opportunity proves that—but keep the respect by listening, learning as you go, and by treading carefully or slowly when necessary. That way, you will not make the mistake of assuming your leadership position like a bull in a china shop, which will leave you with pieces of people and projects scattered everywhere and lots of damage control to undertake before you can move forward again.

To the reluctant leader, I say, "Get with it! Yes, you can! Come out of the shadows and into the light!" Come with boldness; come

> *Chin up, back straight, gaze fixed on the task before you. You must not underestimate yourself or your abilities. You must take your place.*

with confidence; come with courage, knowing that God is on your side. It is He who has called you; He who has equipped you; and He who has appointed you to lead in this hour. Open your eyes to what He sees in you because when He looks upon you, He sees a leader. There is a seat at the head of the table for you and you are more than able to fill it or it would not have your name on it. Chin up, back straight, gaze fixed on the task before you. You must not underestimate yourself or your abilities. You must take your place.

## *You're On*

*1.* Have you saturated your life with prayer as you step into the challenges of leadership? How will you begin to pray about yourself as a leader and about your leadership position?

*2.* What do you believe are the three most important character qualities of a leader? How are you doing in each of these areas? What will you do to improve?

> *A leader is not necessarily someone who has a large ministry or is in a position that influences thousands of people's lives. A leader is someone who is on top of things in his or her realm of influence.*
>
> Joyce Meyer[1]

**3.** What is the best leadership lesson you have learned from someone in your life? How will you incorporate that as you begin to lead?

# *Learn Your Lines*

*Look, the Lord your God has set the land before you;*
*go up and possess it, as the Lord of your fathers has spoken to you;*
*do not fear or be discouraged.*

**Deuteronomy 1:21**

*Only be strong and very courageous, that you may observe to do*
*according to all the law which Moses My servant commanded you;*
*do not turn from it to the right hand or to the left,*
*that you may prosper wherever you go.*

**Joshua 1:7**

*For we are His workmanship, created in Christ Jesus for good works,*
*which God prepared beforehand that we should walk in them.*

**Ephesians 2:10**

## *Act 2: Developing as a Leader*

No matter how many wonderful things there are about you and your leadership (and there are many), you will always have room for improvement. I believe that one of the marks of a true leader is that he or she is eager to grow and develop. There are probably hundreds of leadership tools at your disposal and I encourage you to take advantage of and glean from as many as you can. For now, here are 15 brief suggestions to help you get started down the road to leadership development.

*1.* Be informed. Stay on top of people, places, and events in your industry.

*2.* Affiliate with professional societies or groups within your profession and join key civic organizations.

*3.* Keep your credentials current. Take extra classes.

*4.* Attend seminars and conferences on leadership and about your industry.

*5.* Network. Network. Network.

*6.* Delegate. Delegate. Delegate.

*7.* Surround yourself with other leaders.

*8.* Live a disciplined, balanced life.

*9.* Know your employees and seek to be an excellent example to them.

*10.* Find a mentor.

*11.* Find someone to mentor.

*12.* Always be looking to learn.

*13.* Make the most of technology.

*14.* Set goals and reach them.

> *No matter how many wonderful things are true about you and your leadership (and there are many), you will always have room for improvement.*

*15.* Give yourself, as a leader, a regular progress report. Identify weaknesses and strategies to improve.

## *You're On*

*1.* Have you surrounded yourself with wise counsel while you are developing as a leader? If not, who will you look to as advisers and mentors?

*2.* As your influence increases, so do your responsibilities. How are you going to manage your growing workload?

*3.* Have you identified the future leaders who are currently under your influence? How are you mentoring them?

# *Learn Your Lines*

*If you have run with the footmen, and they have wearied you,*
*then how can you contend with horses? And if in the land of peace,*
*in which you trusted, they wearied you, then how will you do in the*
*floodplain of the Jordan?*
**Jeremiah 12:5**

*And let us not grow weary while doing good,*
*for in due season we shall reap if we do not lose heart.*
**Galatians 6:9**

*So Moses' father-in-law said to him, "The thing that you do is not*
*good. Both you and these people will surely wear yourselves out;*
*you are not able to perform it by yourself. Listen now to my voice;*
*I will give you counsel, and God will be with you . . ."*
**Exodus 18:17, 18**

## *Act 3: Handling Success*

I want to warn you of something you may not have considered as you are rising to new heights of success. Sometimes, challenges arise in relationships when a person begins to enjoy significant achievements. Most of those problems are somehow rooted in the jealousy of other people. Sometimes friends become distant, co-workers become envious, family becomes resentful—all because they are jealous of the woman's talents, or her promotion, or the fact that she is less available to them, or even of God's favor upon her life! And so, leading lady, success draws more out of you than what it takes to appear successful to the world. It reaches down into your soul and draws out the grace to deal with those around you when they

> *Great*
> *people do daily*
> *what other people*
> *do occasionally.*
> Paula White[2]

105

do not understand, or when they reject you, or when their eyes are green with envy. I have but two words for you as you keep moving onward and upward in spite of people's opinions: love and grace. Understand that their struggles with your success are born of their own woundedness and weakness. You are not likely to change their minds, but you can love them anyway, and you can be gracious in every way you can think of. They may come around when they see how much you love them still, but if they don't, they will never be able to accuse you of anything but the greatest gift of all—love!

Those of you who are married may face a unique challenge when you begin to succeed, because unless you are married to a very secure man, your husband may feel threatened, intimidated, jealous, or even devalued by your success. I would like to simply list seven things that will help you navigate your marriage well as you become more and more successful.

*Success draws more out of you than what it takes to appear successful to the world. It reaches down into your soul and draws out the grace to deal with those around you...*

*1.* Maintain good boundaries between your personal life and your professional life. Leave your work at the office and keep your heart at home.

*2.* Affirm your husband verbally. Praise his strong points and thank him for the contributions he makes to your life. Avoid reciting a litany of his weaknesses.

*3.* Do not allow others to make statements that degrade or demean your husband.

*4.* Even if your husband's job and interests do not produce the same financial benefits as yours, stay interested in what he does and participate with him as often as possible.

*5.* Find a financial philosophy that the two of you can agree upon. Determine who writes what checks, what money is allotted to specific purposes, etc.

*6.* Honor your husband as your God-given covering.

*7.* Refuse to allow your professional life to steal from your personal time with your husband.

## *You're On*

*1.* How are you personally going to deal with other people's criticism or jealousy of your success?

*2.* What boundaries do you need to draw around your success? Think about relationships, finances, gifts, time management, and other aspects of your life that will be affected by your success.

*3.* Who can you bless as a result of your success and how?

## *Learn Your Lines*

*Every good and every perfect gift is from above,*
*and comes down from the Father of lights,*
*with whom there is no variation or shadow of turning.*

**James 1:17**

*So it shall be, when the Lord your God brings you into the land of*
*which He swore to your fathers, to Abraham, Isaac, and Jacob, to give*
*you large and beautiful cities which you did not build, houses full of*
*good things, which you did not fill, hewn-out wells which you did not*
*dig, vineyards and olive trees which you did not plant—when you have*
*eaten and are full—then beware, lest you forget the Lord who brought*
*you out of the land of Egypt, out of the house of bondage.*

**Deuteronomy 6:10–12**

*And you shall remember the Lord your God, for it is He*
*who gives you power to get wealth, that He may establish*
*His covenant which He swore to your fathers, as it is this day.*

**Deuteronomy 8:18**

# Coming Soon

$\mathscr{L}$ady, you made it! You have climbed up your chosen mountain and earned a place at the top. Along the way, you've learned some lessons—and you've paid the price to be called a success. Now that you have attained one of your life's great dreams, what else are you dreaming of? Do you dream now of success in another arena, or do you dream of relaxing and enjoying the benefits of what you have accomplished? Since you are successful, chances are that you are also diligent and focused—and perhaps you do not stop and dream the way you once did. Wouldn't you like to do that now?

_____

_____

_____

_____

_____

_____

_____

_____

_____

_____

# ACTION!

*B*ased on what you have learned in this chapter, what are three concise, measurable, attainable goals you will set for yourself as a leader? Be sure to include a schedule and target date for reaching each goal and a reward for accomplishing it.

*1.* Goal:
Schedule and target completion date:
Reward:

*2.* Goal:
Schedule and target completion date:
Reward:

*3.* Goal:
Schedule and target completion date:
Reward:

# Your Finances

# 9

# *The Lady and Her Pocketbook*

## <u>*Introducing*</u>

leading lady knows how to manage her life, and part of her life management includes being a good steward of her resources and knowing how to handle money. A leading lady is secure enough to live within her means, smart enough to budget, and wise enough to stick with the budget once she has it in place. Whether your goal right now is to pay off debt, save for a house, invest for retirement, or simply stop living hand-to-mouth, the principles in this chapter can help get you on a firm financial foundation.

## <u>*The Main Event*</u>

### *Act 1: Making Wise Spending Decisions*

When you consider your money, you probably think about how you spend it. You may think about savings or investments, but I feel that somewhere in your thought process is the issue of what you get with the money at your disposal.

Leading ladies seek wisdom in every area of life and the area of spending is no exception. If you spend wisely, you should have enough to do all of the things that are important to you. Following are some guidelines for spending your money in a manner consistent with wisdom:

> *If you make money your god it will plague you like the devil.*
>
> Henry Fielding[1]

*1.* Pay off the past, be prudent in the present, and prepare for the days to come.

*2.* Learn to tell the difference between what you need and what you want.

*3.* Spend your money wisely. Do not waste it on lottery tickets or games of chance. Do not gamble.

*4.* Keep a written record of the money you spend. Add up your expenditures and see if you are wasting money on things you could do without.

*5.* Think about this: $3 per day for a latte might seem like a harmless indulgence, but by the end of the year, you will have spent more than $1,000 on coffee!

*6.* Always, always, always get a receipt.

*7.* Know where your money goes. Save your receipts and keep track of your spending in a budget log.

*8.* Give up the ATM card (it can make your money hard to track because forgetting to record purchases and withdrawals is so easy to do!)

*9.* Learn the joy of delayed gratification. There is a unique pleasure in waiting to buy something until you can afford it and being able to pay cash.

*10.* Understand that discipline is one of the qualities of a disciple. This includes discipline in the area of finances!

# You're On

*1.* With "1" being just plain stupid and "10" being the height of wisdom, how wise are you when it comes to spending your money?

*2.* Unless you scored a perfect "10" on the previous question, what three steps can you take this week to make better spending decisions?

*3.* In what area of your life are you most likely to overspend? Clothes? Shoes? Jewelry? Cosmetics? How can you discipline and strengthen yourself in that weak area?

*Learn to tell the difference between what you need and what you want.*

**4.** Are you losing money by not recording ATM transactions? If so, how about cutting up that ATM card until you learn to keep track of your funds?

## *Learn Your Lines*

*And my God shall supply all your need according to His riches in glory by Christ Jesus.*
**Philippians 4:19**

*The wisdom of the prudent is to understand his way.*
**Proverbs 14:8**

*Behold, I send you out as sheep in the midst of wolves. Therefore be as wise as serpents and as gentle as doves.*
**Matthew 10:16**

### *Act 2: It's in the Budget!*

The only way to take charge of your spending and enforce the priorities of your lifestyle is to develop a budget and stick to it. Some people cringe when they hear the word *budget*, but it really is the most effective tool for managing your income in a way that will allow you to reach your financial goals and be able to do the things that are important to you.

In his book, *Priceless*, financial guru Dave Ramsey quotes J.W. Fulbright, who said: "Priorities are reflected in the things we spend money on. Far from being a dry accounting of bookkeepers, a nation's budget is full of moral implications; it tells what a society cares about and tells what it does not care about; it tells what its values are.[2]" What is true for nations is also true for individuals. You will give your money to the things you care about and if you do not make the decision to direct your money toward that which you value, you will end up discovering your values by the entries in your checkbook!

When it comes to priorities, I need to tell you that your first order of business needs to be paying God. Tithing (giving one-tenth of your income) is a biblical principle, but it is also a privilege and an act of worship. Tithing allows us to keep everything in proper perspective and to remember that God is our source, the one who provides for us and gives us everything we have. Give your tithe to your home church and then, if you desire to support other ministries, let that giving be an offering (above and beyond your tithe).

*Tithing (giving one-tenth of your income) is a biblical principle, but it is also a privilege and an act of worship.*

Next, pay yourself. Determine your long-term financial goals and put aside a specific amount of money each month as you save for those things. If you do not save the money before you begin paying your bills, chances are that it will be gone. Again, a budget helps you enforce your priorities, so if you have made a priority of sending your children to college, you must set aside money for that purpose before you use your funds for something else.

After you have given your tithe and saved for those top priorities, take care of your other obligations.

I have included an excellent budget worksheet for you in Appendix B of this workbook. I hope you will use it, cut it out of the book, and put it in a place you are likely to see it often (because then you will be reminded to live by it).

## *You're On*

*1.* You knew this question was coming: Do you have a budget?

*2.* What is the purpose of a budget? If you do not have one, will you commit to develop and live by a budget? If not, do you need someone to help you? If so, who will you ask? If not, what are you waiting for?

*Only 8% of evangelical Christians tithe. Can you imagine what would happen if the other 92% started tithing this Sunday? Welfare in North America could be wiped out in 90 days. There would be no church debt or hospital debt in 90 days. You see, when you handle money God's way, you get God's economics.[3]*

*3.* Do you tithe? Why or why not? The attitude of your heart is important in this matter and you need to be able to articulate your reason(s) for giving to God or withholding from Him.

*4.* Are you getting and keeping up with your receipts? If not, what kind of system do you need to implement in order to help you?

# *Learn Your Lines*

*"For which of you, intending to build a tower, does not sit down first and count the cost, whether he has enough to finish it —"*

**Luke 14:28**

*"Bring all the tithes into the storehouse, that there may be food in my house, and try Me now in this," says the Lord of Hosts, "If I will not open for you the windows of heaven and pour out for you such a blessing that there will not be room enough to receive it."*

**Malachi 3:10**

*He who tills his land will have plenty of bread, but he who follows frivolity will have poverty enough.*

**Proverbs 28:19**

# COMING SOON

*I*n order to be a true leading lady, you need to be walking in victory over your finances. I could almost hear some of you say, "Ouch!" the minute you saw the word budget. But let me assure you that a budget is one of the best things you can do as you look toward your future and think about being able to live your dreams. Unless you are a very unusual lady, your dreams are likely to need some funding! Use the space below to write down what you would like to see in the area of budgeting and managing your money. Be sure to include the things you would like to be able to afford to do, but cannot right now.

_____

_____

_____

_____

_____

_____

_____

_____

_____

_____

_____

_____

# ACTION!

*B*ased on what you have learned in this chapter, what are three concise, measurable, attainable goals you will set for yourself in the area of spending? Be sure to include a schedule and target date for reaching each goal and a reward for accomplishing it.

*1.* Goal:
Schedule and target completion date:
Reward:

*2.* Goal:
Schedule and target completion date:
Reward:

*3.* Goal:
Schedule and target completion date:
Reward:

# 10

# The Lady and Her Bills

## Introducing

The main reason people get into financial trouble is that they allow themselves to get caught in the debt trap. So many people don't know how to handle delayed gratification. We are bombarded with the new, the flashy, and the up-to-date, and we buy into the message that we must have the latest fad or fashion now. We have forgotten how to scrimp and save. We run up credit card debt for things that we can't afford so that we will be able to keep up with the Jones family. The burden of debt has become so great for many that filing for bankruptcy has become an acceptable and commonplace escape hatch instead of an option that was once considered late in the game only after other recourses were exhausted.

The bottom line when it comes to credit and debt is to live within your means. Regardless of your situation right now, I hope the information in this chapter will help you climb out of the pit of debt and stay out for good. Your life is too valuable to be hindered by constantly worry about paying bills, and I don't want you to be caught in the web of debt while your destiny is beckoning!

# *The Main Event*

## *Act 1: Know Why You Owe*

Overspending is a symptom, not a cause. I would like to help you probe your own thoughts and examine your spending behavior to see if you can understand the real reasons your mailbox is full of bills, and so many entries in your check ledger list checks to creditors. Here is the truth: your ability to handle money is often a reflection of your security and wholeness as a person. Sometimes women over-spend in a fit of fury over a break-up with a boyfriend. Sometimes they purchase things they can't afford because they feel inferior to others or are trying to impress them. Sometimes a woman is so deeply wounded by traumas in her past that she tries to medicate her pain with the things that money can buy. Then again, we occa-sionally see a relatively whole, stable, secure woman who simply has a problem controlling her credit card.

*Once you understand yourself and your reasons for spending, determine what lifestyle you can afford and stick to it.*

I want to encourage you to gaze into yourself and think about why you are in debt. It may take a while to sort that out, but only when you understand what motivates your spending can you begin to reverse harmful patterns and enforce lasting change. Once you understand yourself and your reasons for spending, determine what lifestyle you can afford and stick to it. Do not be swayed by other people's opinions or by feelings of low self-worth. Listen, lady, you will soon learn if you haven't already, that nothing you bring home in a shopping bag can heal the hurts inside. Maybe it will numb them for a very short time, but they always begin to throb again. If you are in this situation, may I suggest that you read my book, *Woman, Thou Art Loosed.* Countless women just like you have been immensely blessed, helped, and set free by its message.

## *You're On*

*1.* Are you an emotional spender? What emotions trigger the desire to buy something? Have you overextended yourself in order to buy things that you think will impress other people or make you feel that people like or accept you?

*2.* Have you gotten yourself into debt trying to buy things that will make you feel better about yourself? In your own words, why have you spent money you did not have?

> *Your ability to handle money is often a reflection of your security and wholeness as a person.*

*3.* Tell the truth: is your use of credit out of control? How will you reduce your dependence on or overuse of credit? Will you cut up your credit cards?

*4.* Is it really worth an extra twenty or twenty-five percent to buy something immediately when you can wait, pay cash, and only give up the sticker price?

## *Learn Your Lines*

*A faithful man will abound with blessings,*
*but he who hastens to be rich will not go unpunished.*
**Proverbs 28:20**

*Give me neither poverty nor riches —*
*feed me with the food allotted to me.*
**Proverbs 30:8**

## Act 2: The Truth About Credit

In her book, *Financially Secure*, Deborah McNaughton writes, "Every woman should have credit of her own. With so many women in the workforce, it's even more critical that women obtain and manage their own credit. What do creditors look for? Basically, they want to make sure that you can repay any debts you incur and that you do so in a responsible and timely manner."[1]

McNaughton continues, "How do creditors figure out your capacity for debt? They use a standard formula called a debt to income ratio. They start out by calculating your total monthly debt or expenses, which includes your rent or mortgage payments, car payments, insurance, credit card payments, alimony, child support, and so on. When figuring this number, creditors include the monthly payment of the item that you want to finance. Next, they'll divide this number by your total monthly gross (before taxes) income. If the debt ratio is more than 50 percent, most likely you will be denied credit. The total monthly payments divided by the total monthly gross income equals your debt ratio. Before you apply for credit, speak with the lending institution about its debt to income policies."[2]

> *The typical credit card holder carries seven cards with average balances of $1,642. That's more than $11,000 in debt!*[3]

Here are a few pieces of good advice and things you need to know when it comes to credit:

◆ Put away or destroy your credit cards if you cannot withstand the temptation to use them to overspend.

◆ Be prudent about the way you use credit. Do not accumulate a balance that is equal to your credit limit.

◆ Always pay more than the minimum amount due on your bills. Let paying the minimum be an exception rather than your standard operating procedure.

◆ Remember that interest accrues on bills when you do not pay it in full. Not paying bills in full will result in paying only interest every month and never really reducing the primary amount you owe.

◆ Always remember that when you use credit, you will pay the lender back with interest, which means that you will pay back not only the amount you borrowed, but also a specific percentage of that amount. You can pay up to 20 percent interest or more on credit card balances these days.

◆ There are two kinds of interest you are likely to encounter in your financial dealings: simple interest and compound interest. Deborah Owens explains that simple interest is "the interest that is calculated using a simple method, it is calculated at the end of the period. To calculate the interest earned on $1,000 earning 6 percent in a year, simply multiply $1,000 by .06. The result is $60 interest per year of simple interest."[3] She defines compound interest as "the interest that is paid or received on interest from prior periods."[4] This means that your interest will build up and that you will probably end up paying more interest than you thought you would!

## *You're On*

*1.* How much (total) do you owe creditors?

*2.* How much interest do you pay on your three highest-balance credit cards? Do the math: how much money is that per month? Per year?

*3.* How can you begin to eliminate some of the interest you are paying?

## *Learn Your Lines*

*Do not be one of those who shakes hands in a pledge, one of those who is surety for debts; if you have nothing with which to pay, why should he take your bed from under you?*

**Proverbs 22:26, 27**

*The rich rules over the poor, and the borrower is servant to the lender.*

**Proverbs 22:7**

*Then she came and told the man of God and he said, "Go, sell the oil and pay your debt; and you and your sons live on the rest."*

**2 Kings 4:7**

## *Act 3:*
## *Your Credit Report and What It Means*

Deborah McNaughton defines a credit report as "essentially a summary document that tracks how you use your credit" and tells us that "three credit reporting agencies collect this information within the United States: Equifax, Experian, and Trans Union."[6]

She continues, "Creditors credit report information. After you've been granted credit, permission to report your charge and payment habits is included in the creditor's standard terms and disclosures, which you agree to when you accept the credit. From there you are constantly being observed for how you shop, how much debt you incur, how much of your overall debt you pay off, whether you pay on time, what types of credit you use, and so on. That's why it's important to pay your bills on time and to communicate with your lenders when there's a problem because all of this information will affect you at some point."[7]

*Whether you're single or married, you need to obtain a copy of your [credit] report on a six-month to yearly basis.*[10]

"In addition to creditors," McNaughton further informs us, "the reporting agencies will use other sources to gather information on your credit habits. Public records such as tax liens, bankruptcies, judgments, and other public notices are closely watched. For instance, if you become overwhelmed by debt and decide to file for bankruptcy, the credit reporting agencies will report the filing on your credit report."[8]

There is one item on your credit report that is extremely important to understand because it carries such weight with lenders: your FICO score. In essence, this score will tell a lender quickly how creditworthy you are. Your credit report and your FICO score are the two documents a creditor will examine when you apply for a credit card or a loan.

Your FICO score is calculated using several variables that include but are not limited to these:

◆ Total amount of credit you already have

◆ Number of credit inquiries within the past year

◆ Payment history

◆ Amounts owed

◆ Length of credit history

◆ Types of credit used

This information is averaged into a three-digit number. The scores can range from 300 to 900. Most lenders prefer to see a score of 700 or above for credit approval but scores of above 620 will still get good rates.[9]

## *Supporting Roles*

To obtain a copy of your credit report, contact the credit reporting agencies.

| Equifax | Experian | Trans Union |
|---------|----------|-------------|
| P.O. Box 105873 | P.O. Box 2104 | P.O. Box 1000 |
| Atlanta, GA 30348 | Allen, TX 75013-2104 | Chester, PA 19022 |
| 800-685-1111 | 888-397-3742 | 800-888-4213 |
| www.equifax.com | www.experian.com | www.tuc.com |

**To see what your FICO score is, go to
www.myfico.com or www.eloan.com.**

# *You're On*

*1.* Have you ever requested a copy of your credit report? If not, when will you do so?

*75%
of Forbes'
400 said, when
surveyed, that the
number one key to
building wealth
is to be debt-
free.*[11]

*2.* If your credit rating is not good according to your credit report, what steps will you take to improve it? (You may want to make this one of your goals.)

*3.* Do you need to consider credit counseling? (If so, there are a variety of agencies. Be sure to use one that is reputable. You can start by researching these agencies on the internet.) (You may want to make this one of your goals.)

# *Learn Your Lines*

*A good name is to be chosen rather than great riches.*

**Proverbs 22:1**

*The wicked borrows and does not repay,*
*but the righteous shows mercy and gives.*

**Psalm 37:21**

*Better not to vow than to vow and not pay.*

**Ecclesiastes 5:5**

*Will not your creditors rise up suddenly? Will they not awaken*
*who oppress you? And you will become their booty.*

**Habakkuk 2:7**

In order to help you plan to pay off your debt, I have included a debt-elimination worksheet in Appendix C. Please use it; then cut it out, and put it in a place where you can see it often—that should inspire you!

# COMING SOON

*In* order to enjoy your life as a leading lady, you really do not need to be tied to a credit card. I tell you, that little piece of plastic can weigh fifteen tons! If you have ever experienced the exhilaration of dropping that last payment in the mailbox, you know what I mean when I say that reducing debt can be addictive! Once you start seeing those balances drop to zero and stop seeing bills piling up in front of you, you just cannot help being driven to eliminate your debt. Just imagine what you can do when your money is not always going to pay a bill! Just imagine what you can do when you can make your own decisions about spending, saving, or investing it. Go ahead, use the space provided and just imagine . . .

# ACTION!

*B*ased on what you have learned in this chapter, what are three concise, measurable, attainable goals you will set for yourself in the area of credit and debt-reduction? Be sure to include a schedule and target date for reaching each goal and a reward for accomplishing it.

*1.* Goal:
Schedule and target completion date:
Reward:

*2.* Goal:
Schedule and target completion date:
Reward:

*3.* Goal:
Schedule and target completion date:
Reward:

# 11

# The Lady and the Long Term

## Introducing

Lady, I believe that you have lived long enough by now to know that the things you want do not just drop out of the sky. No, life takes planning. When it comes to your finances, it is wise to keep one eye focused on the present and the other gazing toward the future. There will come a day when you do not receive the paycheck you have now or when you cannot depend upon your spouse's income to be what it is currently. So you must think ahead now, do your best to anticipate your future needs and wants, and develop a sound financial strategy for the long term.

By the time you are ready to retire, you will have worked hard and made significant contributions to the world. You're going to want to relax and enjoy life, and with smart planning now, your golden years can truly shine!

# *The Main Event*

## *Act 1: The Importance of Investing*

Deborah Owens writes in *Confident Investing* that, "Investing keeps you moving ahead financially instead of stalling. If your money is standing still, you're falling behind. The cost of things you need and want is going up every day. If your money isn't being invested so that it creates more money and enables you to keep up, the money that you have will not be enough for what you need and want."[1]

She adds that, investing is your best chance to . . .

◆ Make career moves that are good for you.

◆ Start your own business.

◆ Contribute to your parents' lives, if you choose, without it being a burden.

◆ Send your kids to college.

◆ Go to college yourself.

◆ Stop working for a salary and start working for personal enjoyment instead.

◆ Pursue your dreams, not just a paycheck.[2]

Owens understands how important it is for women to invest: "Women generally live longer than men. Someone must pay for your care in your later years. If you have the money to make the choice, you'll choose to live in quality. If you don't, someone else will choose who will care for you and where. Investing can help you have enough to live the way you want to at the end of your life."[3]

She also understands that "life is unpredictable. We go into it believing that we have control over almost everything in our lives, and then it happens—a surprise that lights our fire or rocks our boat. We win an award, we get fired, our parents split, friends take us on a cruise, the college that we chose doesn't choose us, we have twins, companies go under, the biopsy is positive, our car insurance wasn't renewed after all."[4]

She informs us that, "as women, 90 percent of us will be solely in charge of our finances at some point in our lives. This means that we will experience life changes. We will marry, probably more than once, have children, survive our partner, or be responsible for the care of a parent or relative."[5]

She makes the interesting observation that, "we will also evolve as people with passions that surface and beg for expression. We will want the money to go to New Mexico on a photographic mission. We will want to contribute time and money to the outdoor camp for troubled kids that helped our grandchild. Facing life changes is easier with enough money. Investing can help you have enough."[6]

*The cost of things you need and want is going up every day.*

I think Deborah Owens has undertaken some of the same projects I have. How can I tell? Because she says, "You know how it is when you plan a vacation or remodel a room. It nearly always costs more than you thought it would. Even more certain, living your life—even a life of simplicity—will cost more than you think it will. Investing keeps your money growing so that you can keep up with rising costs. Not only are costs of today's products increasing, but breakthroughs in medicine and technology are also producing incredible products that will enhance and improve our lives. You'll want enough money to benefit from them."[7]

Owens succinctly sums up the need to invest: "You'll need more money than you think you will to live, give, and love well for the rest of your life."[8]

# *You're On*

*1.* Do you currently have any investments? Are you adding to your investments regularly?

*2.* Are you comfortable with your investments?

*3.* Why is it personally important for you to be a smart investor?

> As women, 90% of us will be solely in charge of our finances at some point in our lives.

# *Learn Your Lines*

*For the kingdom of heaven is like a man traveling to a far country, who called his servants and delivered his goods to them. And to one he gave five talents, to another two, and to another one, to each according to his own ability; and immediately he went on a journey. Then he who had received the five talents went and traded with them, and made another five talents. And likewise he who had received two gained two more also. But he who had received one went and dug in the ground, and hid his lord's money. After a long time the lord of those servants came and settled accounts with them. So he who had received five talents came and brought five other talents, saying, "Lord, you delivered to me five talents; look, I have gained five more talents besides them." His lord* said to him, "Well done, good and faithful servant; you were faithful over a few things, I will make you ruler over many things. Enter into the joy of your lord." He also who had received two talents came and said, "Lord, you delivered to me two talents; look, I have gained two more talents besides them." His lord said to him, "Well done, good and faithful servant; you have been faithful over a few things, I will make you ruler over many things. Enter into the joy of your lord." Then he who had received the one talent came and said, "Lord, I knew you to be a hard man, reaping where you have not sown, and gathering where you have not scattered seed. And I was afraid, and went and hid your talent in the ground. Look, there you have what is yours."

*Matthew 25:14–25*

## Act 2: Understanding Investments

I really want you to understand some of the language of the investment world. As you consider investing your money, there are certain basic terms you need to know. I have grouped them into categories: investing/long-term/retirement planning, and paying for your child's education. I want to thank Deborah Owens for allowing me to use these definitions from her book, *Confident Investing*. You will find all these and more on pages 265–286 of her excellent resource.

### Investing / Long-term / Retirement Planning

**401(k):** A tax-qualified retirement plan for employees of for-profit companies. Employees can contribute a percentage of earned income by payroll deduction. The employer can contribute to the employee's contributions, based on a percentage of earnings.

**403(b):** A tax-qualified retirement plan for employees of non-profit companies, such as schools, churches, and municipalities. Employees can contribute a percentage of earned income by payroll deduction.

The employer can contribute to the employee's account or match the employee's contributions, based on a percentage of earnings.

*Adjusted gross income:* Taken from the individual's income tax return, this term means total annual income, minus tax-exempt income, minus other adjustments to income such as deductible IRA contributions and self-employed health insurance premiums.

> *Not only are costs of today's products increasing, but breakthroughs in medicine and technology are producing incredible products that will enhance and improve our lives. You'll want enough money to benefit from them.*

*Annual report:* A company's annual report to shareholders. This report includes information about finances, management, and operations. All publicly traded companies must submit this report to the SEC annually. This annual SEC filing is known as the 10-K report.

*Annuities:* A contract between an insurance company and an individual; annuities provide tax-deferred growth and income to the investor. Generally, in return for either a lump-sum payment or a series of payments, the company will guarantee an income stream, typically for the annuitant's lifetime or some other specific period.

*Asset:* Any possession that has value upon exchange.

*Asset allocation:* A rational process of diversification of an investor's assets among different asset classes, taking into account all characteristics of the investor's financial situation and investment objectives.

**Bond:** A fixed-income security that is a legal obligation of the issuing company or government to repay the loan principal to bondholders on a specified date. In addition, the issuer promises to pay interest to the bondholder at a rate stated on the face of the bond certificate.

**Diversification:** The investment practice of not keeping all your eggs in one basket. Diversification across asset classes and within asset classes reduces unsystematic risk and portfolio volatility.

**Dividend:** A share of after-tax company earnings that is paid to share-holders of record. Most dividends are paid in cash but are sometimes paid in additional shares of stock of the same or a different company. Dividends are declared quarterly by the company board of directors.

**Financial statement:** A statement of financial values that represents cash flow or net worth of an individual or company.

**Investor:** A person who buys or sells securities for his own accounts or the accounts of others.

**Liquid Assets:** Cash or other assets that can be easily converted into cash.

**Pension plan:** Typically a defined-benefit retirement plan.

**Portfolio:** A combination of invested assets; the combined investment holdings of an investor.

**Qualified retirement plan:** An employer-sponsored retirement plan that receives privileged income tax treatment by the IRS. All employee contributions are made with before-tax dollars, meaning that income tax is not currently paid on any contributions. Employer contributions made to employee accounts are currently tax-deductible to the employer. Account earnings accumulate on a tax-deferred basis, meaning that no income tax is paid until withdrawals are taken from the account, usually during retirement. Withdrawals taken before age 59½ are subject to a 10 percent excise tax penalty in addition to regular income tax treatment, with limited exceptions.

*SEP IRA:* A qualified retirement plan for a small business of 25 employees or fewer. Contributions to each employee's individual SEP IRA account can be made by the employer on a tax-deductible basis. Employee contributions are made on a pre-tax basis, typically by payroll deduction, as a percentage of income. Assets accumulate on a tax-deferred basis. IRS limitations pertaining to early withdrawal penalties apply.

*Simple IRA:* A qualified retirement account for small businesses or self-employed individuals. The employee can contribute a maximum of $6,000 per year on a before-tax basis; the employer can contribute up to three percent of employee compensation on a tax-deductible basis. Assets accumulate on a tax-deferred basis. IRS limitations pertaining to early withdrawal penalties apply.

*Stock:* An instrument that certifies a proportionate unit of ownership in a corporation.

*Stock dividend:* New shares of stock that are distributed to shareholders as a dividend. This can be in addition to a cash dividend or in lieu of a cash dividend. It can be stock of the dividend-issuing company or stock of another company, usually a subsidiary of the issuing company.

**Stock market:** An organized marketplace where securities are bought and sold on behalf of investors.

**Taxable income:** Net income that is taxed; for individuals, adjusted gross income, minus itemized deductions, minus personal exemptions equals taxable income.

**U.S. Savings bonds:** Bonds that are issued by the U.S. Department of the Treasury and backed by the full faith and credit of the United States government.

**Vesting:** A term that is used regarding qualified retirement plan accounts; an ERISA guideline that requires that an employee be entitled to all retirement benefits upon leaving employment after a certain number of years of service.

## Paying for Your Child's Education

**Education IRA:** An IRA for use in educational planning. A maximum contribution of $500 per year per student under age 18 can be made. Contributions are not income tax-deductible, but earnings accumulate on a tax-deferred basis and are tax-free if used for education, including tuition, books, or room and board. There are income limitations for tax-free withdrawals.

**Pell Grant:** A needs-based grant for undergraduate students. It is the first level of funding of the financial aid package; other federal and private aid is added to it. Because the Pell Grant is a grant, it does not need to be paid back. The maximum award for the 2002–2003 award year was $4,000. The Pell Grant is awarded to all eligible students, but the amounts for future awards will depend on program funding.

**Perkins loan:** A low-interest (5 percent) loan available to both under-graduate and graduate students who have exceptional financial need. This need is determined by a federal formula using the information provided on the Free Application for Federal Student Aid (FAFSA). The loan is made with government funds, but the school is the lender.

*Don't use the money in your IRA or 401(k) plan unless you absolutely have to. There is a penalty for withdrawing the money before age 59½. You are putting this money away for your old age. Letting it grow is a very good idea. Pretend you don't even have it.*[9]

**Student Aid Report:** The Student Aid Report (SAR) is received a couple of weeks after the Free Application for Federal Student Aid (FAFSA) is mailed to the processor. The SAR contains all the information provided on the FAFSA, messages from the processor, and some calculations. Upon receipt, the SAR should be reviewed to make sure that all of the information is correct.

**Student Loan Marketing Association (SLMA):** A non-profit organization that buys student loans from many lenders and packages the loans to students in an effort to help students consolidate their loans into a single, more affordable loan. The SLMA sells packaged student loan portfolios to investors as a fixed-income security. Also known as "Sallie Mae."

# *Supporting Roles*

For more information, visit the following internet sites:
**www.collegescholarships.com** and **www.petersons.com/finaid/**

# *You're On*

*1.* What is a 401(k)? If applicable, are you participating fully in the plan that your employer offers?

*2.* What is an IRA? Do you have any IRAs? If not, which type of IRA makes the most sense for you?

*3.* What is a stock? Are you investing in the market? What about a bond? Do you have any bonds? Could one or both of these options make financial sense for you?

*4.* Do you have a child or children to send to college? If so, what are you doing to prepare for that expense?

## *Learn Your Lines*

*Owe no one anything except to love one another . . .*
**Romans 13:8a**

(And realize that providing for those you care about is an expression of love!)

# COMING SOON

*I*'ve said it before, most dreams need funding. Unless something very unusual happens, you will need money in the days to come and you will need it long after you want to keep working for it—that's called retirement. Your retirement should be a rich and rewarding season, but you will need to plan for it. As you think about your long-term financial strategy, what dreams do you want to be able to afford?

_____

_____

_____

_____

_____

_____

_____

_____

_____

_____

_____

_____

_____

# ACTION!

$\mathcal{B}$ased on what you have learned in this chapter, what are three concise, measurable, attainable goals you will set for yourself in the area of investing and maximizing your hard-earned money? Be sure to include a schedule and target date for reaching each goal and a reward for accomplishing it.

*1.* Goal:
Schedule and target completion date:
Reward:

*2.* Goal:
Schedule and target completion date:
Reward:

*3.* Goal:
Schedule and target completion date:
Reward:

# 12

# The Lady and Her Team

*I would like to thank Deborah Owens for the content of this chapter. Much of the substance you will read below comes from her book,* Confident Investing, *pages 226–227.*

## Introducing

f you're like millions of other people, you work hard and try to save as much as possible. That's good because there will be milestones in your financial life: college for you, your children, or all of you; caring for aging parents or loved ones; a second career; and either full or partial retirement. But how do you successfully pass each of these milestones and get to where you want to be? That's right—by using an adviser [or team of advisers].[1]

The bottom line on selecting an advisory team is to do your homework, make your selection, and stick with the people you select. There is no substitute for preparation, and because the people you select will probably be your guides for some time, you should do as much preparing and interviewing as needed until you find the right fit for your situation.[2]

# The Main Event

## Act 1: How an Adviser Can Help

Here are some of the advantages of using an adviser or an advisory team. All of this information is taken directly from pages 226–227 of *Confident Investing* by Deborah Owens.

### Vast Number of Products

The vast number of products/investment vehicles and incredible array of mutual funds, stocks, bonds, and other investments can cause analysis paralysis if you're doing it without help. An adviser can help you navigate this minefield.

### Specialized Knowledge

Sometimes you can really lose money by being a "do-it-yourselfer." Preparing your own taxes is one example. Your tax situation may be simple enough, but you may miss a new deduction or strategy. What you don't know can cost you.

Another example is insurance. Owning the right types and amounts of insurance is extremely important. Do you know if you have what you need? There are many uses of insurance besides paying a death benefit when someone dies. Insurance can be used to make investments, make up for lost wages if you are temporarily unable to work, and protect your loved ones from undue tax penalties upon your death, to name a few. An adviser provides the specialized knowledge that "do-it-yourselfers" need but don't have.

*A financial advisory team has four basic jobs: (1) Create and grow wealth for you. (2) Protect and preserve your wealth. (3) Plan for the most tax-advantaged distribution of wealth during life. (4) Plan for the most tax-advantaged distribution of wealth at death.[5]*

### Clearer Path

An effective adviser will keep you moving on the path you've chosen. Achieving your financial milestones requires the accumulation of wealth, and that requires much preparation, thought, and following through. The decisions that you make and the actions that you take will make a tremendous difference in whether you reach your life goals. The right adviser can help you reach them.

### Your Team

Establishing a team with whom you can have a good rapport, trust, and open discussion is something that you can do for yourself over time, if not immediately. Your team might include a financial planner who acts as a "quarterback," a stockbroker, an accountant, an insurance agent, and an attorney.

### Why a team?

A team gives you a wide perspective on the choices you will make. Members of your financial team may even disagree to a point. The value they bring is giving you more than one way to view your choices. Ultimately, you will make the decisions, but your advisers will provide information that will help you make the best decision for each situation.

## *You're On*

*1.* What financial needs or situations do you need help with immediately?

*2.* Which of the advantages listed above do you think will be most valuable to you?

*3.* From which friends or associates will you solicit recommendations for your advisers?

# *Learn Your Lines*

*Where there is no counsel, the people fall;*
*but in the multitude of counselors there is safety.*
**Proverbs 11:14**

*Plans are established by counsel . . .*
**Proverbs 20:18**

## *Act 2: Qualities of an Effective Adviser*
*All of this information is taken from* Confident Investing, *pages 228–230. Greater detail is available there as well.*

### Trustworthiness

Trustworthiness is first because it is the foundation for your relationship with your financial adviser. All the good looks, smooth talk, and letters behind her last name on her business card don't mean much if you don't have faith in what she's telling you. Having trust and faith means having a comfortable feeling about the path you're on; not having it means questioning almost everything that your adviser recommends. Because your financial journey lasts a lifetime, be certain that you trust the adviser(s) you're bringing with you on the trip.

### The Ability to Educate

A good adviser must be an educator. Most people who are good at their profession possess this trait. A good teacher communicates well and is willing to explain something more than once and in more than one way if necessary. Remember, advisers have gone to school to learn what they know. Expect an adviser to translate terms and concepts to you in ways that you can grasp, and never be afraid to ask a question more than once.

### Listening Ability

You must be able to fully express your goals, fears, hopes, dreams, and present financial situation. Your adviser should listen, take notes, ask questions, and then give you feedback on what you just said. Only then can your adviser start to fully understand where you are now and where you want to go, and then formulate a plan to get you there.

### Communication Skills

An effective adviser not only listens, but she also gives feedback, offering insight and clarity. An adviser in any field must translate the language and concepts to the client. In the case of a financial adviser, she will interpret the language and concepts of the financial industry, and, in terms you can understand, explain how each investment recommended will contribute to your portfolio as a whole.

### Objectivity

Objectivity is crucial in choosing investments. Just because a certain stock or mutual fund has performed well and is the "hot pick" of the moment doesn't mean that it's right for you. A good financial adviser keeps current on new financial products and updated on products already being sold, viewing them objectively with you in mind.

A good financial adviser also doesn't let the amount of commissions paid to her influence her suggestions about what investments will ultimately be chosen for your portfolio.

### Competence

Competence may seem like an obvious qualification to you, but it's not always obvious that an adviser is incompetent. Just because someone says she's been a financial adviser for a period of years, doesn't mean that she knows what she should know and can do her job at a high level.

Owens informs us that, "The financial industry has standards that each adviser must meet. These standards help ensure that a minimum level of service is provided to each client. One of the best ways to make sure that the person you choose is competent is through professional designations."[4]

Professional designations include:
RR  – Registered representative with a brokerage house
RIA – Registered investment adviser
CFP – Certified financial planner
CPA – Certified public accountant
CLU – Certified life underwriter (for your insurance needs)
PFA – Personal financial adviser[5]

In addition to a financial adviser or team of advisers, you may have need of an attorney at some point. You will want to look for the same qualities I have just shared in a lawyer, just as you would seek them in a person who helps you with your finances. Sometimes people feel that attorneys can be intimidating, so I would like to share with you one lawyer's version of a client's Bill of Rights.[6]

*1.* The client shall set the objectives of the representation and make all business decisions involved in the representation.

*2.* The client is entitled to a full discussion and explanation of any legal strategy proposed by her lawyer.

*3.* The client is entitled to prompt and responsive representation. All client phone calls should be returned by the lawyer within 24 hours.

*4.* The client is entitled to regular progress reports on all pending matters.

*5.* The client is entitled to an honest assessment of the time required to complete a task and an adherence to reasonable deadlines.

*6.* The client is entitled to clear, detailed, and accurate billing.

*7.* The client is entitled to complete confidentiality of all information learned by the lawyer during the representation.

*8.* The client is entitled to full disclosure from the lawyer of all settlement offers and contract proposals.

*9.* The client is entitled to full disclosure of any potential conflicts of interest the lawyer may have.

*10.* The client is entitled to integrity and honesty from the lawyer.

> *A good financial adviser will also help you understand whatever investments you may already own.*[7]

## *You're On*

*1.* What is most important to you in a financial adviser?

> *An adviser who educates you will lead you to your best solutions.*[8]

*2.* If you are married, have you and your husband discussed the things you will need to know in the event of his death? Do you have the right attorney and financial advisory team in place? If not, when will you do so?

*3.* In the case of divorce, do you have an attorney and a team of financial advisers you trust? Who are they?

*4.* In the event that you inherit money or property, do you have an adviser you trust? Who is it?

## *Learn Your Lines*

*The heart of the prudent acquires knowledge,*
*and the ear of the wise seeks knowledge.*
**Proverbs 18:15**

*He who has knowledge spares his words,*
*and a man of understanding is of a calm spirit.*
**Proverbs 17:27**

### *Act 3: Interviewing an Adviser*

I find Deborah Owens' advice on choosing an investment professional, or a team of professionals, especially helpful. "You may not have had the experience of hiring someone before. Meeting with and choosing a prospective adviser is not something that should be done quickly or without preparation. During the interview, you may get a "gut" reaction about the person you're talking with, but you shouldn't jump to conclusions or make on-the-spot decisions. Ask the same questions of everyone you meet with, take notes, and then carefully make your choice."[9]

She continues, "Always interview at least three people for each type of adviser you need. This is a good rule that should not be broken. Why? Because you will learn from each person you talk with, even though you're asking the same questions. Also, each adviser you interview may be from a different company and have different methods of creating plans and different methods of getting paid for their services. You can always interview more than three, but you should never interview less."[10]

### *Sample Adviser Interview Questions*

*All sample interview questions are taken from* Confident Investing, *pages 235–237.*

*1.* What is your educational background? Most advisers have college degrees, and some have a master of business administration (MBA) degree, but don't be too impressed by this. It's true that if someone has a master's degree, that person has learned more specialized information than someone with a bachelor's degree. Of course, the degree should be in the area of business, because an engineer usually doesn't learn about advanced investment strategies in college.

*2.* What are your credentials? In other words, what has this adviser accomplished?

*3.* What is your background and experience? How long have you been an adviser? Have you worked continuously for the same firm? Do you have a working knowledge of a broad range of investment products, or have you specialized in one particular investment such as bonds?

*4.* What type of clients do you advise? An adviser may have limited the business to only commercial clients with 401(k) plans. Also, some advisers take on only "high-end" clients with $500,000 or more of assets in their accounts.

*5.* What type of financial plans do you create? Are the plans for one particular event, such as retirement, or do you create plans that include savings for life events, such as college and retirement? How many pages and how many illustrations do your plans usually contain? Your goal is to have a thorough, concise plan. Make sure you get and pay for only what you really need.

*6.* How often do you meet with clients? It's important for you to know how often the adviser reviews client accounts. Many advisers review their clients' accounts daily just to see how certain investments are performing. They don't change investments; they just keep an eye on things. Periodic meetings with clients keep an adviser informed of any events in the client's life, such as the birth of a child, which may affect how a portfolio is invested. Periodic meetings also keep you, the client, educated on how your account is growing and keep you involved in the wealth-building process.

*Remember, you are the one hiring the adviser, so you get to decide who to hire according to your own criteria.[11]*

*7.* How are you compensated? You must decide whether you want a fee-only adviser who will create your plan but let you make the investments, or whether you want someone to "tend your garden" and have an active involvement in building your wealth.

*8.* Do you have any current clients that I could talk to? Talking with current clients is a great way to find out how an adviser performs on the job.

## You're On

Don't you think we've had enough questions for this section?

## Learn Your Lines

*Counsel in the heart of man is like deep water,*
*but a man of understanding will draw it out.*
**Proverbs 20:5**

*A scoffer seeks wisdom and does not find it,*
*but knowledge is easy to him who understands.*
**Proverbs 14:6**

# COMING SOON

*L*ady, one of the marks of a leader is that she knows when and where to go when there are other people whose expertise exceeds her own in certain areas. Perhaps this chapter has caused you to consider doing some things you had not thought about when it comes to putting together a winning team to help you with your finances and investments. What kind of team do you envision? What character traits are important to you in the people who help you handle your money? What do you want to accomplish with them in your corner? Bear in mind that these may be the very people you call when you face tragedy or crisis. They will also be the ones for whom you are grateful when your future is secure!

_____

_____

_____

_____

_____

_____

_____

_____

_____

_____

_____

_____

# ACTION!

*B*ased on what you have learned in this chapter, what are three concise, measurable, attainable goals you will set for yourself in putting together an effective team of financial advisers? Be sure to include a schedule and target date for reaching each goal and a reward for accomplishing it.

*1.* Goal:
   Schedule and target completion date:
   Reward:

*2.* Goal:
   Schedule and target completion date:
   Reward:

*3.* Goal:
   Schedule and target completion date:
   Reward:

# 13

# The Lady and the Big Bucks

## Introducing

This is exciting. You've got your financial act together and you are ready to put down a significant chunk of change to buy a new car or even a home! But as exciting as it is, these large outlays of money can be confusing as you navigate your way through salespeople, lending institutions, and legal matters. You may hear car-buying terms or real estate language you have not heard before, and that is one reason I include this chapter for you. Furthermore, there is much to learn about such expensive purchases. There are many auxiliary costs to consider once you get beyond making the purchase and into the land of being a car owner or a homeowner. I want to make sure that you understand not only the relatively short buying process, but the long-term commitment you make when you buy a car or a house.

I can hear the jingle of keys in the distance! I rejoice with you that you have come to this point in your life and pray that you walk wisely through the process!

# *The Main Event*

## *Act 1: Are You Ready?*

In the previous chapter, we tried hard to help you know how to build a trustworthy, competent team of people to help you with financial matters, primarily your investments. But it is also smart to surround yourself with good counsel when you make a major purchase. The automobile market, and especially the housing market, can be quite complex, so it is wise to work with people who have some expertise in these fields. Unless you are an expert yourself, part of getting ready to buy a house or a car will be surrounding yourself with a few people who really know what they are doing in these areas—people you trust and who do not stand to gain anything as a result of your purchase.

When you think about being ready to make a major purchase, you must look beyond simply having the necessary down payment in hand and consider the whole of your financial situation. Your primary concern should be the effect of your purchase on your overall budget. You don't want to "rob Peter to pay Paul!" Both of those guys have to be paid, so in other words, do not allow the monthly payments (if you have to make them) and the additional costs of owning a house or a car, cause you to be spread so thin financially that you struggle to meet other obligations. If you feel this could happen, I encourage you to wait on your major purchase until it fits more comfortably into your budget.

I have mentioned several times the additional costs involved in being a car owner or a homeowner. Fees and charges vary, but let me mention just some of those so that you will know specifically what I am talking about. With a car, you will pay taxes, fees for registration and license plates, possibly a destination charge, gasoline, and routine maintenance, which is critical to keep your car running well. In addition, you may have a "surprise" repair bill that is not covered under warranty or, in the event that you have an accident, there may be the payment of an insurance deductible. With your home, you will have closing costs, fees for realtors, moving expenses, homeowner's insurance, association fees (for condominium complexes and some neighborhoods), possible unexpected repairs, and a whole host of other situations that will cost money. All of these things must be considered when you are deciding whether or not you are ready to make a major purchase.

## *You're On*

*1.* Are you prepared financially to make a major purchase such as a house or a car?

*2.* Do you have advisers or experts (who do not benefit financially from the transaction) who can help you with these big decisions? Who are they?

> *When you think about being ready to make a major purchase, you must look beyond simply having the necessary down payment in hand and consider the whole of your financial situation.*

*3.* Are you prepared to take on the responsibilities that come with a major purchase—insurance, maintenance, etc.?

*4.* Trying to impress people or to "keep up with the Joneses" is a horrible reason to buy a car or a house. Is there any such desire in you as you consider your purchase? If so, deal with that now.

*5.* Why do you think you are ready to make a major purchase?

## *Learn Your Lines*

*Be diligent to know the state of your flocks,*
*and attend to your herds; for riches are not forever . . .*
**Proverbs 27:23, 24**

*The plans of the diligent lead surely to plenty,*
*but those of everyone who is hasty, surely to poverty.*
**Proverbs 21:5**

## Act 2: A New Set of Wheels

Unless you have saved enough money to buy the new car you really want, or are willing to settle for a car for which you can pay cash, you will probably need to finance your automobile purchase. Pay as much as possible on a down payment so that you can finance as little as possible.

You may have had your eye on a particular make or model for a long time, or you may not be sure what kind of car you want. I can only suggest two criteria for choosing your car: make sure it meets your needs (a two-door convertible is not practical for a woman with toddlers and three car seats to accommodate!), and make sure you do not pay more than you absolutely must. You will have to determine your own needs, but once you have identified the vehicle or type of vehicle you will buy, then shop around. Test drive various models and consider consulting *Consumer Reports* magazine (they have an entire issue devoted to cars and it is very helpful when you are trying to choose a car). If you are intimidated by salespeople, non-confrontational, or simply uneducated when it comes to car prices, take someone with you—take the best negotiator you know!

*Once your car is paid off, take the money you were making on car payments, and put it into a special account. Let the money build up so that when it is time to purchase a new car, you will be able to pay cash and need no financing help.*[6]

Some dealerships have adopted a no-hassle, one-price-take-it-or-leave-it, policy, but other dealerships can and will negotiate. Some will even beat a competitor's price if you take it to them in writing. You can also find out a lot of helpful negotiating information on the internet and in magazines. Until you are completely satisfied with a reasonable price that you and the dealer agree upon, keep picking up your purse and walking off that lot.

Deborah McNaughton, in *Financially Secure*, offers some helpful advice about car shopping. "When you fill out a loan application, the lender will consider your debt to income ratio. Most banks will offer loan packages to people whose debt is between 35 and 38 percent of their income. This is not a hard-and-fast rule, however. Because you want to keep credit inquiries to a minimum, check with the finance manager at the car dealership before submitting an application to determine the criteria for loan qualification. You can also hand carry a recent copy of your credit report with you. Just be sure to protect your information. If you give it to a dealer, chances are, the finance manager will run a check. Too many recent credit inquiries from shopping around will only create credit approval problems for you."[1]

She continues, "Expect the car dealership's finance department to examine your income, employment, residency, and prior credit history. The car dealership will look closely at your car payment history and your FICO score too."[2]

McNaughton further advises us, "Review your credit reports before your car search. Why? Your APR [annual percentage rate of interest] will be based on your credit score. You want the lowest interest rates you can find. In addition to shopping around for the best deal, make sure your application looks good."[3]

Isn't this good advice? Here's more: "When you work with a dealer, understand what you're paying for and why. Don't be afraid to ask questions. For instance, if you're required to put down a deposit, find out whether it's refundable."[4]

Finally, McNaughton concludes, "Likewise, if you have any questions or concerns regarding your contract, ask. For example, will you be assessed penalties for paying off the loan early? Clarify any information you don't understand. Should you have any doubts about anything, get an answer before you sign any paperwork."[5]

## *You're On*

*1.* In the interest of wisdom, do you think you should buy a new car or a previously-owned car?

*2.* How much are you willing to spend on a car?

*3.* Are you hoping that your car will impress others or help you feel better about yourself? If so, proceed with the greatest caution as you buy your car because it will eventually fail you in both cases.

*4.* Can you pay cash for a car with which you would be comfortable?

*5.* If you cannot pay cash, how much car can you really afford? How much will you need to put down in order to keep from overextending yourself with monthly payments?

# *Learn Your Lines*

*Without counsel, plans go awry, but in the multitude
of counselors they are established.*

**Proverbs 15:22**

*Now godliness with contentment is great gain.*

**1 Timothy 6:6**

## *Act 3: Your Castle*

They say a man's home is his castle, but a woman's home is her castle as well. It is the place she lives her life, the one place above all others that should reflect and celebrate who she is. It is a place of prayer and worship, of intimate moments and special gatherings, a place where she expresses herself, rests herself, refreshes herself—and from which she greets the world.

Buying a home is a rite of passage, a mark of adulthood—not to mention a good investment! But there are some things you need to know as you consider purchasing the place of your dreams.

The real estate world has a language of its own, so here are some definitions that will help you understand and communicate within it. They are all taken directly from Deborah McNaughton's book, *Financially Secure*, pages 180–181.

*FICO scores are important in qualifying for a mortgage. Ask the lender how high your score must be to get the best interest rates and how low it can be to qualify.*[11]

**Term of loan:** This is the time it will take to pay off the mortgage. Generally the industry standard is thirty years, but you can find fifteen and twenty-five year options, too.

**Fixed rate:** Your interest rate will remain the same throughout the life of the mortgage.

**Adjustable rate mortgage (ARM):** Initially your interest rate will start out low, often one to two points lower than a fixed rate (based on the current economy). Rates are then adjusted; the terms of a loan set forth a timetable. Most rate adjustments occur between six and twelve months. The benefit of adjusted rates is that if the market rates fall, so will your monthly payment.

**Rate cap:** With an ARM, it's typical to establish a cap, or how high your rate can adjust within a given period as well as over the life of the loan. This cap protects you against drastic market changes, but an ARM is not as stable as a fixed-rate.

> *When you're trying to qualify for your house payment, use the general rule of four to one. That is, your monthly payment should not exceed 25 percent of your gross monthly income.*[12]

**Rate reduction:** You can reduce your interest rate by opting for a shorter-term loan. A fifteen-year rate is often 0.25 to 0.5 percent lower than a thirty-year rate. You'll also pay less in the long run because you'll pay less interest (even with the same amount) due to the shorter loan length.

**Prepayment penalty:** If there is a prepayment penalty on your loan, it will be disclosed in the note you sign with the lender. You will have to pay a penalty if you prepay the loan balance before a certain period of time (mentioned in your note).

You are not limited to a bank as your only lending institution when buying a house. Research your options in terms of types of loans that are available and in terms of lenders, which will include banks, credit unions, mortgage companies, and savings and loans. Also, check the internet, as there on are on-line services as well.

All lenders require you to fill out a standardized application, frequently referred to as a 1003 (a Fannie Mae designation). Your application should reflect current and complete information. Items on your credit report should confirm information you note on your application. Be prepared to provide the following:

◆ W-2s for the past two years

◆ Year-to-date pay stubs

◆ Current debt information (account numbers, balances, creditors' addresses)

◆ The purchase contract for the home you want to buy

◆ Tax returns for the past two years

◆ Bank statements for the past three months

◆ Any statements for a 401(k) or IRA accounts, or other investment information listing assets

◆ Copy of divorce papers; documents about child support and alimony

◆ Copies of any past bankruptcy papers[7]

In addition, here are some more tips to remember as you travel the road that leads to home.

Make sure all financial information you disclose is accurate and complete.

Lenders will regard positively a change in position to better yourself financially. On the other hand, having breaks in employment every couple of months and switching business fields will raise flags.[8]

While you're going through the process and up until the time funds are disbursed, do not make any changes to your financial situation (buying a major appliance or a car, changing jobs, opening new credit card accounts, etc.).[9]

The property you want to buy must be appraised. A lender will offer only a percentage of the property-appraised value.[10]

Buying a house can be a long, involved, expensive, and even harrowing process. But there is no feeling in the world like closing the door after the last box has been delivered and knowing you are home. I wish you well, leading lady. I wish you the home of your dreams and the wisdom to know how and when to purchase it. And I wish you much happiness there!

## *You're On*

*1.* Have you seriously considered all of the expense involved in buying a house? Have you seriously considered all of the expense involved in owning a house?

*2.* Is now the time for you to buy, or should you stay where you are until you have saved additional money toward the purchase of a home?

*3.* Buying a house is an enormous investment. Have you sought wise counsel and are you convinced through prayer that you are doing the right thing?

*4.* Have you thoroughly investigated your options regarding financ-‘ing and do you know your rights and responsibilities as a buyer?

*5.* What part of buying a house gives you reason to pause? Can you overcome that?

## *Learn Your Lines*

*Through wisdom a house is built, and by understanding*
*it is established; by knowledge rooms are filled*
*with all precious and pleasant riches.*

**Proverbs 24:3, 4**

*The wise woman builds her house,*
*but the foolish pulls it down with her hands.*

**Proverbs 14:1**

*The house of the wicked will be overthrown,*
*but the tent of the upright will flourish.*

**Proverbs 14:11**

*Unless the Lord builds the house, they labor in vain who build it.*

**Psalm 127:1**

# COMING SOON

One thing is true about leading ladies—they can take care of themselves, as long as they have surrounded themselves with good advisers! They can make big decisions and smart decisions and they can manage their lives and their money effectively. When you dream of making large purchases, what goes through your mind? Especially when it comes to your home, what kind of place do you dream about and what do you envision happening within those walls?

_____

_____

_____

_____

_____

_____

_____

_____

_____

_____

_____

_____

_____

# ACTION!

$\mathcal{B}$ased on what you have learned in this chapter, what are three concise, measurable, attainable goals you will set for yourself as you plan ahead for your future? Be sure to include a schedule and target date for reaching each goal and a reward for accomplishing it.

*1.* Goal:
   Schedule and target completion date:
   Reward:

*2.* Goal:
   Schedule and target completion date:
   Reward:

*3.* Goal:
   Schedule and target completion date:
   Reward:

# Your Health and Appearance

# 14

# The Lady at the Table

## Introducing

Leading ladies know that in order to succeed in life, you need to be healthy. You can help yourself immensely by eating right, and by feeding your body what it needs. If you think of your body as a machine, your food is its fuel. Now, you don't want your insides clogged up with fat and grease and junk, do you? You want to fuel yourself with things that will give you energy and keep your body in good working order, right? After all, your body is God's gift to you and it is the temple of His Spirit in you. You don't want to fill the temple with worthless idols, do you?

## The Main Event

### Act 1: You Are What You Eat

The U.S. Department of Agriculture has its famous "food pyramid" and recommends the following foods in the following amounts each day.

- Bread, cereal, rice, and pasta: 6–11 servings

- Vegetables: 3–5 servings

- Fruits: 2–4 servings

- Milk, yogurt, and cheese: 2–3 servings

- Meat, poultry, fish, dry beans, eggs, and nuts: 2–3 servings

- Fats and oils: use sparingly

When I determined to lose weight and eat a healthier diet, I began working with my friend, health designer and chef, Carlo Gabrelian. But I didn't start working with him in order to help myself; I started because I wanted to help free some time in my wife's busy schedule. But before long, he shared with me some tips for healthy living, and I want to pass them along to you because they are excellent guidelines to remember as you choose your foods.

- Eat three meals and two snacks every three hours every day.

- Eat 70% of your calories by 2:00 in the afternoon.

- Eat most of your carbohydrates for lunch.

- Eat mostly protein for dinner.

- Quit eating by 7:00 at night.

- Exercise at least four hours a week.

- Never do two hard things at the same time.

- Never put two bad foods together in the same meal.[1]

# *You're On*

*1.* What is the best thing about your eating habits? What is the worst?

*2.* What is the most important change you can make in your eating habits?

*3.* How are you going to begin to eat in a healthier way?

For some healthy recipes, please turn to Appendix D.

# *Learn Your Lines*

*But He answered and said, "It is written: 'Man shall not live by bread alone, but by every word that proceeds from the mouth of God.'"*

**Matthew 4:4**

*I know that nothing is better for them than to rejoice, and do good in their lives, and also that every man should eat and drink and enjoy the good of all his labor—it is the gift of God.*

**Ecclesiastes 3:12, 13**

*Have you found honey? Eat only as much as you need, lest you be filled with it and vomit.*

**Proverbs 25:16**

## *Act 2: Fast the Fast Food!*

Lady, I want to make sure you know that fast food is one of your body's greatest enemies and that you should get on the warpath against it. Fast food is loaded with calories, saturated fat, and sodium—all of which are bad for you. Avoid fried hamburgers, fried chicken, and french fries as much as possible, eating instead fresh fruits and vegetables, lean meats that are baked, broiled, or grilled and whole grain breads instead of white.

There are always days when your morning is so hectic you forget to take the lunch you packed, and there are other days when unexpected situations arise and going through a fast-food drive-thru is your best option. For those times, here is *Reader's Digest's* list of the ten healthiest choices you can make at several fast food restaurants.

*To maintain a healthy weight and lower your risk of heart disease, get no more than 30 percent of your daily calories from fat, no more than 10 percent from saturated fat, and less than 300 milligrams of dietary cholesterol per day. Ideally, eat at least five servings of fruits and vegetables per day, and eat foods from other plant sources (such as grains) each day.*[2]

*1.* Burger King Chicken Whopper Jr. (hold the mayo)

*2.* Domino's Classic Hand-Tossed Cheese Pizza with fresh vegetables (two medium slices)

*3.* Hardee's Hamburger

*4.* Jack in the Box Hamburger

*5.* KFC Tender Roast Sandwich (hold the sauce)

*6.* McDonald's Grilled Chicken Caesar Salad with fat-free Herb Vinaigrette dressing

*7.* Pizza Hut The New Edge Veggie Lover's Pizza (two slices)

*8.* Subway any of the "Under 6" sandwiches or salads

*9.* Taco Bell Chicken Soft Taco

*10.* Wendy's Small Chili (without cheese)[3]

# *Supporting Roles*

**For fast food nutritional counts, use the internet and go to:**
**http://dietriot.com/fff/rest.html**

Now, here are some excellent ideas for healthy lunches and snacks. These are taken from *The Little Blue Book of Fitness and Health.*[4]

◆ Experiment with healthy substitutes for your favorite foods such as mustard and salsa rather than mayonnaise, and ground turkey instead of hamburger (#9).

◆ Need a quick snack? Grab a bagel or even a baked potato. Both steadily supply energy in the form of starches and are easy to carry on the go (#13).

◆ Kiwi, papaya, cantaloupe, strawberry, mango, orange, and tangerine are all packed with calcium, folic acid, iron, protein, and vitamins (#34).

◆ Substitute applesauce for shortening when baking (#44).

◆ Pack a lunch that includes carrot sticks and an apple (#52).

◆ Cabbage is packed with vitamin C, potassium, folic acid, and fiber. Make a tasty coleslaw with shredded carrots, onions, mustard, and a smidgen of low-fat mayonnaise or dressing (#55).

*A 16-ounce Coca-Cola contains 198 calories.*[5]

◆ A handful of dried fruits and nuts makes a quick, energy-boosting snack. Be careful not to overindulge, however, because they're high in calories (#64).

◆ Clean and slice carrots and celery, and put them into a plastic container in the fridge so that they'll be ready for a quick snack (#66).

◆ Create main dishes that feature pasta, rice, beans, or vegetables. Mix those foods with small amounts of lean meat, poultry, or fish (#69).

◆ Vegetables such as peas, corn, and potatoes are nutritious—but if you're keeping track of food groups, remember that they count as carbohydrates (#70).

◆ Using a vegetable steamer is a delicious way to prepare vegetables—and it retains many of the vegetables' nutrients as well (#75).

◆ Read nutrition labels. The most important information is serving size, fat, and calories. Your doctor can recommend appropriate calorie and fat levels (#96).

◆ There is no cholesterol in grains, nuts, fruits, or vegetables. It's found only in animal products (#101).

◆ Salmon, sardines, herring, mackerel, cod, and haddock are packed with protein—and a type of healthy fat with lots of heart-healthy benefits (#113).

◆ For inexpensive, nutritious, and low-fat protein, try beans, split peas, and lentils. You can buy them cooked or easily prepare the dried variety (# 119).

◆ Choose pretzels over potato chips (#149).

◆ Water is nature's soft drink (#151).

◆ Enjoy pasta with red sauce. Avoid or limit Alfredo, cream, and buttery sauces (#159).

◆ Remove turkey and chicken skin—it's loaded with fat. When possible, choose white meat over red meat (#161).

◆ Bananas might be nature's most perfect food (#171).

## *You're On*

*1.* How many times per week do you eat fast food? How much money do you spend per week on fast food?

*2.* If you order lunch at the drive-through purely for the convenience factor during a busy work day, what can you do to make it easier to prepare your own lunch and have healthy foods for lunch?

*One super size order of McDonald's french fries contains more calories than any of their hamburgers.*

*3.* If you were really committed to healthy eating, which specific fast foods would you need to eliminate from your diet? Which restaurants would you not visit anymore?

# *Learn Your Lines*

*. . . and make no provision for the flesh, to fulfill its lusts.*
**Romans 13:14**

*Beloved, I beg you as sojourners and pilgrims,*
*abstain from fleshly lusts, which war against the soul.*
**1 Peter 2:11**

## *Act 3: Lay Aside the Weight*

So many women struggle with their weight. Whether they never dropped those pregnancy pounds, or the extra inches crept up on their waist over a period of years, they are almost always eager to enjoy the health and appearance benefits of losing weight.

Most health guides recommend that highly active people of normal weight who want to keep from gaining more should limit their calories to 2,400 calories a day with no more than 25% of their total calories in fat. This would be about 67 grams of fat per day. If a person wants to lose weight gradually, the nutritionists recommend that women eat between 20 and 40 grams of fat a day.[7]

You will have to determine how you will lose the weight that needs to leave—whether you will attack the pounds primarily through a change in your diet and moderate exercise or whether you will exercise intensely and make smaller adjustments in your eating habits. For now, I would like to submit to you five truths I have learned about food. I believe they will help you get off to a good start regardless of the way you choose to say goodbye to your extra weight.

> *Know this for truth, and learn to conquer these: Thy belly first, sloth, luxury, and rage. Do nothing base with others or alone, and, above all, thine own self respect.*
> Pythagoras[6]

## *Food Truths*[8]

***Food Truth #1: We must balance our intake of food with our output of energy.***

If we eat too many calories and consume more fat grams than we can use, our body must store the leftover energy somewhere. The body was designed by God to store the extra energy in fat cells. To defeat [the fat giant], we must balance our output of activity with our intake of fuel. If your activity is not demanding enough to necessitate your consumption, you must cut back.

***Food Truth #2: Starvation is not balance.***

If we withhold food from our body, it is designed to shut down its metabolism and conserve energy to extend its life span. Our metabolism works better when it is busy digesting low-fat foods than when it shuts down from starvation. Therefore, give your body frequent supplies (five times per day) of low-fat nutritious food to energize it and to stimulate your metabolism.

***Food Truth #3: Your body needs four hours of exercise each week.***

Balancing exercise with sensible eating keeps the fat giant from rising up against you again. Remember: More food is all right, but it is going to mean more strenuous activity. You would be shocked at how much walking or how many sit-ups it takes to burn off that fried chicken! After a while, you will conclude it is not worth it.

*Here is a sample of what you could have in three meals and two snacks:*

<u>Breakfast:</u> *Cereal with skim milk and a banana.*

<u>Morning</u> <u>snack:</u> *any snack with carbohydrates.*

<u>Lunch:</u> *Any pasta with green salad and fat-free dressing.*

<u>Afternoon</u> <u>snack:</u> *Apple and fat-free pudding.*

<u>Dinner:</u> *Chicken breast with any kind of salad or green vegetables.*[9]

**Food Truth #4: Believing the truth will save your life, your dream, and your ministry.**

Face the facts, believe the truth, and stick to it. The greatest weapon is information, and when you have the truth, do not allow your temptation to dull your convictions. You must have health and energy for anything you want to do with your life. Your strength is dependent on the fuel you feed your body.

**Food Truth #5: Spirit-filled living is better than self-control.**

If you walk in the Spirit, you will not fulfill the lust of the flesh (see Galatians 5:16). Any time we are Spirit-controlled, we are personally empowered. As believers, we are to become disciples of Jesus Christ. Discipline, which is following the Spirit of God instead of our flesh, brings our behavior into alignment with what we believe in the first place. Balance requires a maturity that overpowers desire.

> *Avoid having fellowship or counseling over food. The more engrossed you get in the conversation, the more you eat. Disassociate eating from fellowship. Many times we eat subconsciously because we do it while we are doing something else.[10]*

## *You're On*

*1.* How much weight have you gained in the past five or ten years? Are you ready to drop those pounds?

*2.* Which approach do you think will work best for you: lots of exercise while slightly adjusting your eating habits, or an extremely disciplined diet with moderate exercise?

*3.* Are you an emotional eater? If so, how can you vent or deal with your emotions in a way that does not involve food?

## *Learn Your Lines*

*Therefore we also, since we are surrounded by so great a cloud of witnesses, let us lay aside every weight, and the sin which so easily ensnares us, and let us run with endurance the race that is set before us.*

**Hebrews 12:1**

*I say then: Walk in the Spirit,*
*and you shall not fulfill the lusts of the flesh.*

**Galatians 5:16**

# COMING SOON

*L*eading ladies need to be healthy in every way and proper nutrition is essential to good health. What do you need or want to do in the near future in order to feed your body well? Think also about how much better you will feel when you eliminate the excess fat and/or sugar in your diet and when you are feeding yourself with the fuel your body needs. Take a minute to dream on paper about how you will feel and what you will do with all that energy!

_____

_____

_____

_____

_____

_____

_____

_____

_____

_____

_____

_____

# ACTION!

*B*ased on what you have learned in this chapter, what are three concise, measurable, attainable goals you will set for yourself in the area of nutrition? Be sure to include a schedule and target date for reaching each goal and a reward for accomplishing it.

*1.* Goal:
   Schedule and target completion date:
   Reward:

*2.* Goal:
   Schedule and target completion date:
   Reward:

*3.* Goal:
   Schedule and target completion date:
   Reward:

# 15

# The Lady and Two Important Issues

## Introducing

omen's health is a field all its own and I cannot pretend to understand it personally! I have simply been related to and observed enough women to know that there are lots of unique issues women face. There are some issues that affect more women than men, two of which are eating disorders and struggles with depression and/or anxiety. My only goal in this chapter is to raise your awareness of these conditions and alert you to some of their indicators. It just may be that, because you are informed, someone you love will get the help they need. If you observe the symptoms in someone, please consult a medical professional.

## The Main Event

### Act 1: Eating Disorders

We live in an image-conscious society, surrounded by magazines and media that seem to want us to believe that nothing but thin is beautiful. An alarming number of women, especially young women, suffer from some sort of eating disorder and though this workbook is not the place for extensive information on such conditions, I would like to take an opportunity to define three of the most common eating disorders and to list some of their symptoms.

All of the lists of symptoms come from the Diagnostic and Statistical Manual of Mental Disorders of the American Psychiatric Association, as reprinted in *All About Eve.*[1]

### Anorexia Nervosa

Author Tracy Chutorian Semler writes that anorexia nervosa, "commonly called just 'anorexia', this eating disorder often takes hold in adolescence or young adulthood and is characterized by self-starvation and dangerous weight loss."[2] In *All About Eve,* she includes the following things to look for if you think someone may be anorexic.

### Danger Signs

◆ Refusal to maintain body weight at or above a minimally normal weight for age and height

◆ Weight loss leading to body weight less than 85% of that expected

◆ Failure to make expected weight gain during a period of growth, leading to body weight less than 85% of that expected

◆ Intense fear of gaining weight or becoming fat, even though underweight

◆ Disturbance in the way one's body weight or shape is experienced, undue influence of body shape and weight on self-evaluation, or denial of the seriousness of current low body weight[3]

### Other Warnings

◆ A downy fuzz of hairiness on the face or arms

◆ A preoccupation with cooking, food preparation for others; peculiar habits in handling food

◆ Frequent weighing of themselves, perhaps before and after exercise

◆ Complaints of feeling bloated or nauseated after eating normal amounts of food

◆ Irritability, difficulty concentrating, withdrawal, turning inward, depression

◆ Tendency to bruise easily

◆ Fatigue

◆ Eating miniscule portions of food at meals, if eating at all

◆ Sometimes, trips to the bathroom to vomit after meals

◆ Hiding thinness under large, bulky clothes[4]

*About seven million women suffer from eating disorders in the U.S.[10]*

## Bulimia Nervosa

Semler writes that, "Known by most as "bulimia," (from the Greek words for *ox* and *hunger)* this now highly publicized illness . . . consists of cycles of overeating (bingeing) and purging by means of self-induced vomiting and the use of drugs like diuretics, laxatives and other unhealthy methods of cleaning out the body. Bulimics tend to be a bit older than anorexics, often in their later teens, 20s and older, and may be of close-to-normal weight."[5]

## Danger Signs

◆ Recurrent episodes of binge eating

(a) Eating, in a discrete period of time (within any two-hour period, for example) an amount of food that is definitely larger than most people would eat during a similar period of time in similar circumstances

(b) A sense of lack of control over eating during the episode (feeling that one cannot stop eating or control what or how much one is eating)

◆ Recurrent inappropriate compensatory behavior in order to prevent weight gain, such as self-induced vomiting, misuse of laxatives, diuretics or other medications, fasting [unreasonably], or excessive exercise

◆ The binge eating and inappropriate compensatory behaviors both occur, on average, at least two times a week for three months

◆ Self-evaluation is unduly influenced by body shape and weight

◆ Disturbance does not occur exclusively during episodes of anorexia[6]

She explains that there are two different kinds of anorectics:

◆ The restricting type: no binge eating or purging behavior

◆ The binge-eating/purging type: with binge eating, purging, self-induced vomiting, misuse of laxative or diuretics[7]

### Other Warnings

◆ Discolored teeth caused by acid from vomit eroding the enamel

◆ Swollen face, swollen glands

◆ Weight fluctuations, sometimes dramatic, sometimes several times in the course of a year

◆ Calluses on fingers and knuckles due to acid from self-induced vomiting

◆ A very extroverted personality—"I'm having fun and everything's fine"

◆ Eat enormous meals but never seem to get obese

◆ Abuse of alcohol and other drugs

◆ Strict diets followed by excessive eating

◆ Secretive regarding binges—hidden food, hidden laxatives or diuretics

◆ Often use the bathroom after meals to purge; after purging, often appear swollen, agitated

◆ Depressive moods

◆ Overeating in reaction to emotional stress[8]

Semler also informs us that there are two different kinds of bulimics:

◆ The purging type: regular, self-induced vomiting, misuse of laxatives or diuretics

◆ The non-purging type: person uses other inappropriate compensatory behaviors such as fasting or excessive exercise[9]

> *Women with eating disorders are generally more concerned with others' opinions, perceptions, and approval of them. They are often competitive and highly motivated to please others—at the same time, they're often quite dependent on these significant others.[11]*

## You're On

*1.* Do you see any signs of anorexia in yourself or someone you love? What are they?

*2.* Do you see any signs of bulimia in yourself or someone you love? What are they?

*3.* If you see signs of an eating disorder, what action will you take in order to get help?

## *Learn Your Lines*

*Beloved, I pray that you may prosper in all things and be in health, just as your soul prospers.*

3 John 2

## *Supporting Roles*

**National Association of Anorexia Nervosa and Associated Disorders, Inc.**
P.O. Box 7
Highland Park, IL 60035
(708) 831-3438

**American Anorexia/Bulimia Association**
165 W. 46th St.
New York, NY 10036
(212) 575-6200

**Anorexia Nervosa and Related Eating Disorders, Inc.**
P.O. Box 5102
Eugene, OR 97405
(503) 344-1144

## *Act 2: Power, Love, and a Sound Mind*

One of the things believers can rejoice in is that, "God has not given us a spirit of fear, but of power and of love and of a sound mind" (2 Timothy 1:7). Nevertheless, the offices of counselors and clergy people are filled with women who feel hopeless and powerless and even at times like they are going crazy. Depression and anxiety are two common problems for women, so I wanted to mention them in this workbook and to encourage you to get help if you recognize any of the symptoms in yourself or in someone you love.

In *All About Eve,* Tracy Semler writes, "Clinical depression is a strictly defined illness that is believed to be caused by a network of both biomedical and social issues. While many people think depression means feeling sad or blue, it's actually much more complicated than that. We're too quick to use the expression, "I'm so depressed" when we're just feeling down or frustrated. Yes, people with clinical depression might feel sad, but they don't have to feel sad in order to fit the definition of the disorder. Other common feelings of depression include a lack of interest in usual activities, a feeling of being slowed down or tired, and the sense that it's hard to keep going each day."[12] You might also be depressed if you can answer "yes" to any of the questions below.

*1.* Are you depressed or irritable most of the day, most days?

*2.* Do you have a reduced interest or pleasure in most activities, most days?

*3.* Have you gained *or* lost a significant amount of weight or had a significant increase or decrease in your appetite?

*4.* Have you had trouble sleeping . . . *or* are you sleeping too much each day?

*5.* Do you feel either very agitated, *or* like you've slowed down?

*6.* Are you fatigued or have you lost your energy?

*7.* Do you feel worthless, or do you feel inappropriate guilt—that is, do you think about an event or events constantly, blaming yourself, or feeling things are your fault?

*8.* Do you have trouble concentrating or are you being indecisive?

*9.* Do you have recurrent thoughts about death (including your own death) or do you have suicidal thoughts or plans?

Sometimes, women suffer from not only depression, but also some sort of anxiety, too. I'd like to share some information on two anxiety disorders that are especially common in women: generalized anxiety disorder and panic disorder.

Semler writes, "Generalized anxiety disorder [GAD] . . . is characterized by extreme, excessive, irrational chronic worry that impairs one's ability to get through the day and perform normal tasks. The strict definition requires that patients have two different areas of irrational worry over a six-month period. It is seen more often in later-middle-aged women."[13] She continues, "Patients with GAD have trouble concentrating, often startle easily, and have shakiness and palpitations. They seem a little bit like frightened animals, jumpy and unable to function properly."[14]

According to *All About Eve*, "Psychiatrists define a true panic attack as consisting of at least four of the symptoms [listed]. The symptoms usually occur suddenly—in about ten minutes, you'll go from no unusual feelings at all to at least four full-blown panic symptoms. The definition of a panic disorder also requires that at some point, panic attacks occur spontaneously—that is, they are not triggered by an obvious stressor."[15]

*There are 12 to 13 million depressed people in the U.S., and 7 to 8 million of them are women.*[17]

### What a Panic Attack Feels Like[16]

- Heart palpitations
- Shortness of breath
- Choking feeling
- Chest pain or discomfort
- Hot flashes or chills
- Sweating
- Dizziness or lightheadedness
- Nausea/vomiting
- Numbness or tingling
- Feeling like you're having a heart attack
- Feeling like you're going to lose control

*Of those who enter clinics for treatment of panic disorders, 70% are women.*[18]

I want to make sure you understand that both depression and anxiety are common among women and that there is an enormous amount of help available. If, in reading through this section, you can identify with the symptoms mentioned, please seek professional help. Don't let anxiety or depression rob you of another day!

## You're On

*1.* Do you see any signs of depression in yourself or someone you love? What are they?

**2.** Do you see any signs of an anxiety disorder in yourself or someone you love? What are they?

**3.** If you see signs that indicate a need for help, what will you do to get it?

## *Learn Your Lines*

*For God has not given us a spirit of fear,*
*but of power and of love and of a sound mind.*
**2 Timothy 1:7**

*I waited patiently for the Lord; and He inclined to me, and heard my*
*cry. He also brought me up out of a horrible pit, out of the miry clay,*
*and set my feet upon a rock, and established my steps.*
*He has put a new song in my mouth — praise to our God . . .*
**Psalm 40:1–3**

*Be anxious for nothing, but in everything by prayer and supplication,*
*with thanksgiving, let your requests be made known to God;*
*and the peace of God, which surpasses all understanding,*
*will guard your hearts and minds through Christ Jesus.*
**Philippians 4:6, 7**

# Supporting Roles

National Mental Health
Association
Information Center
1021 Prince St.
Alexandria, VA 22314
1-800-969-6642

American Psychiatric
Association
1400 K St. NW
Washington, DC 20005
(202) 682-6000

Anxiety Disorders
Association of America
11900 Park Lawn Dr., Ste. 100
Rockville, MD 20852-2624
(301) 231-9350
www.adaa.org

Rapha
(Christian counseling services
and psychiatric treatment facility)
1-800-383-HOPE
www.raphacare.com

American Psychological
Association
750 1st St. NE
Washington, DC 20002
(202) 336-5500
www.apa.org

National Institute of
Mental Health
500 Fishers Lane
Rockville, MD 20857
1-800-64-PANIC

The Minirth Clinic
(Christian medical and
counseling services)
2100 North Collins Blvd., Ste. 200
Richardson, TX 75080
1-888-646-4784
www.minirthclinic.com

National Depressive and
Manic Depressive Association
730 North Franklin
Chicago, IL 60610
1-800-82-NDMDA
www.ndmda.org

National Anxiety Foundation
3135 Cluster Dr.
Lexington, KY 40517
1-800-755-1576

# COMING SOON

*I*f you have ever struggled with one of the two important issues discussed in this chapter, I say to you again that there is hope for your future! Won't you take a few minutes now to write down your dreams of life once you have conquered an eating disorder, anxiety, or depression?

_____

_____

_____

_____

_____

_____

_____

_____

_____

_____

_____

_____

_____

_____

# ACTION!

$\mathcal{B}$ased on what you have learned in this chapter, what are three concise, measurable, attainable goals you will set for yourself in the area of nutritional and emotional health? Be sure to include a schedule and target date for reaching each goal and a reward for accomplishing it.

*1.* Goal:
Schedule and target completion date:
Reward:

*2.* Goal:
Schedule and target completion date:
Reward:

*3.* Goal:
Schedule and target completion date:
Reward:

# 16

# The Lady Stays Fit

## Introducing

Fitness is crucial for every leading lady, because in one form or another every leading lady has a race to run. She not only needs to be fit for the sake of her physical health, she needs to be fit in order to have the strength and stamina to fulfill God's purposes for her life. We want to glorify Him in our bodies, and one of the best ways to do that is to make sure we exercise, and we do not burn ourselves out by working too long or too hard. God's purposes for you will last until your dying breath and you want to be as fit as you can be for as long as possible so you can continue serving Him with everything you've got!

## The Main Event

### Act 1: Get Moving!

Any amount of exercise is better than none at all, so whatever you do, get moving! Choose exercises you enjoy. If there are none that you enjoy, choose to do them in places you enjoy. Maybe walking in the park might be better for you than walking on a treadmill. Perhaps watching an action movie will make the treadmill more exciting. Try walking with people who want to talk to you. Tell them to hang up the phone and meet you in the park.[1]

Below are some tips and tidbits that will encourage you to start exercising or to improve the work-out program you already have. They are found in *The Little Blue Book of Fitness and Health.*

◆ People who exercise regularly have 36 percent lower health-care costs and 54 percent shorter hospital stays (#1).

◆ Consult a physician before beginning any diet or exercise program (#2).

◆ Don't worry if your weight creeps up when you first start to exercise—muscle is heavier than fat. Instead of watching the scales, notice how your clothes fit (#11).

◆ Stretch, stretch, stretch. Flexible muscles are stronger and less prone to injury (#19).

◆ As a general rule, you should burn 2,000 calories in exercise per week. (Running a mile burns 100-150 calories) (#27).

◆ Enjoy your time in the pool—any movement in water burns one-third more calories than the same movement in air (#40).

◆ Expect some soreness when you begin an exercise program. This is part of the break-down/build-up process that ultimately strengthens the body (#47).

◆ When starting weight training, choose a weight that you can readily lift ten times.

◆ Add weight when you get to where you can finish your sets with relative ease (#54).

◆ Most exercise experts recommend working out at a target heart-rate zone of 70 to 80 percent of your maximum, which is roughly 220 minus your age (#61).

> *Your body appreciates with use. God didn't make your body to wear out with use, like the cars and appliances that depreciate in a few years. God made your body to become stronger and healthier the more you use it.*[5]

- Drink one cup of water for every thirty minutes of exercise (#63).

- Walking is one of the greatest exercises. Walk with your whole body—torso, hips, and legs moving smoothly and easily together, with a rolling heel-toe motion (#82).

- Exercise can help relieve depression and improve self-esteem (#88).

- Trim your inner thighs with a low-intensity, long-term workout such as bicycling or running (#91).

- Try circuit training—rotating to different workout equipment with little rest in between—to beef up your workout and add variety. For best results, rest no more than sixty seconds in between (#106).

- For resistance training when out of town, use rubberized workout bands or portable weights that you fill up with water (#130).

*God is more glorified by living sacrifices than by prematurely dead saints.[2]*

Just a word to those of you who travel: Get the load off of your shoulders! Luggage and laptops and all the things you carry on the plane can be heavy. Carrying such loads as you maneuver through airports (often on the run!) can be bad for your back and neck. Before you step into an airport again, may I encourage you to get a carry-on bag that rolls and one that has a handle long enough for you to roll it comfortably. One woman I know travels all over world with a black nylon backpack on wheels. "It certainly isn't sexy," she says, "but it's the smartest travel tool I've found!"

## *You're On*

*1.* How often do you exercise?

*2.* Why do you personally need to exercise and how will a strong, fit body help you in your everyday life?

*3.* What kind of exercise schedule will you commit to? (Include this in the goals you list under "Action" at the end of this chapter.)

> *If you fall asleep within minutes of hitting the pillow, you're likely sleep-deprived. Most of us need eight to nine hours of sleep a night.[4]*

*4.* What adjustments do you need to make to your lifestyle or routine in order to have a time or a place to exercise? Do you need to trade in some television or telephone time in order to exercise?

*5.* If you were already fit, what would you be doing that you are not doing, or cannot do, currently?

# Learn Your Lines

*I beseech you therefore, brethren, by the mercies of God,*
*that you present your bodies a living sacrifice, holy acceptable to God,*
*which is your reasonable service.*

**Romans 12:1, 2**

*Or do you not know that your body is the temple of the Holy Spirit who*
*is in you, whom you have from God, and you are not your own?*
*Therefore, glorify God in your body and in your spirit, which are God's.*

**1 Corinthians 6:19, 20**

*. . . I have come that they may have life,*
*and that they may have it more abundantly.*

**John 10:10**

## Act 2: Personal Sabbath

If you have walked with God for any time at all, you know that
His plans are perfect. This includes His design for a Sabbath rest
once a week. I know, leading ladies have extremely busy lives and
there never seems to be enough time to do the things you need to do,
much less the things you want to do—and less than that, time for a
break! But I must encourage you to observe a personal Sabbath and
to take a few hours out of your hectic schedule for yourself—time to
rest, time to be refreshed, time to relax, time to remember the joy, and
savor the wonder of life.

The most productive fields are the ones that lie fallow for a season every once in a while. That is because they cannot yield strong
crops year after year after year without being replenished. You are
like the field; you produce and perform and give everything you've
got to the activities of your life. But you will eventually become
drained and unable to give life if you do not stop and rest. Do not

keep going until you are drained; rest and re-fuel regularly so that you maintain a constant rhythm of pouring out, then stopping for a drink. I encourage you to drink deeply from the wells of God's Spirit, for nothing will refresh you like He will. You must take time to be alone with Him and allow Him to minister to your needs and to strengthen you afresh for every task and every challenge you must face as a leading lady.

## *You're On*

*1.* Do you ever take a Sabbath for yourself? What personal benefits do you (or would you) derive from a weekly respite?

*2.* If you are in ministry, you may find it difficult (or impossible) to take a Sabbath rest during the weekend. When do you take your day off?

*3.* What is the most restful, most relaxing, most refreshing things you can think of? If your answer is not realistic as a part of your weekly routine, what is the most restful, relaxing, refreshing thing that is feasible for you on a regular basis? (Save your first answer for a vacation!)

# *Learn Your Lines*

*Remember the Sabbath day, to keep it holy.*
**Exodus 20:8**

*And He said to them, "The Sabbath was made for man,
and not man for the Sabbath."*
**Mark 2:27**

*Speak to the children of Israel, saying: Surely My Sabbaths
you shall keep, for it is a sign between Me and you throughout
your generations, that you may know that I am the Lord who
sanctifies you . . . Work shall be done for six days, but the seventh
is the Sabbath of rest, holy to the Lord. Whoever does any work
on the Sabbath, he shall surely be put to death.*

**Exodus 31:13–15**

*Therefore, since a promise remains of entering His rest,
let us fear lest any of you seem to have come short of it.*

**Hebrews 4:1**

# COMING SOON

*L*eading ladies need to feel good! You need to be strong physically and to make sure you are rested so that you can operate at your optimum all the time. Won't you take a few minutes right now to think about how good you will feel when you are exercising—how much your physical self-image will improve when you are tight and toned, how much more energy you will have, how much better you will look in your clothes? How will you feel about yourself? Dream also about what you will do (or not do!) as you implement a personal Sabbath—how will you spend that time and how do you think you will handle the things you deal with once you are taking a regular break from your stress.

_____

_____

_____

_____

_____

_____

_____

_____

_____

_____

_____

# ACTION!

*B*ased on what you have learned in this chapter, what are three concise, measurable, attainable goals you will set for yourself in the areas of exercise and rest? Be sure to include a schedule and target date for reaching each goal and a reward for accomplishing it.

*1.* Goal:
Schedule and target completion date:
Reward:

*2.* Goal:
Schedule and target completion date:
Reward:

*3.* Goal:
Schedule and target completion date:
Reward:

# 17

# The Lady
# Looks Good

## Introducing

t's amazing what a difference the right clothes, a great haircut, well-applied makeup and some good old-fashioned know-how can make in a woman! If you are going to be a leading lady, you must look like one. We all know that a woman's beauty is not all external, but it does help to be well-groomed and polished because the way you present yourself reflects the way you feel about yourself—and leading ladies know very well how special and how valuable they are. They know they are worth investing in themselves and taking the time and effort required to look their best. After all, isn't that what being a leading lady is all about—being the best in every area of your life?

Whether or not you can afford designer clothes and expensive jewelry is not my concern in this chapter. My only goal is to help you maximize what you do have and help you move down the road toward looking like a million bucks!

# The Main Event

## Act 1: Start with Radiance

You've heard it said that beauty is in the eye of the beholder and, lady, you need to behold yourself and declare yourself beautiful! There is a confidence that simply radiates from a woman who knows she is beautiful, not because of what she sees in the mirror but because of what she gazes upon in her heart. The truth of the matter is that nothing—not designer clothes, not expensive cosmetics or those pumps-to-die-for—will cover up or compensate for a woman who is not radiant on the inside.

> It is who you are on the inside that should define what you choose to do with your outside.[1]

That inner glow comes from the fire in the heart of a woman who knows who she is and Whose she is. That fire is ignited and stoked by her confidence in God and by her unshakable conviction that He loves her. When a lady is grounded in the Father's love, there is a stability about her, a solidness, a security, and a deep, abiding joy that shows up on her face as pure radiance. Once a woman knows Whose she is and knows that nothing and no one can threaten her position as the Lord's beloved, she is then able to hear His voice as He defines her being, as He tells her what is special and unique about her, and as He shares with her the purpose for which He has created her. There is no substitute for the radiance that is born of this kind of relationship with Him and it is the foundation of every true form of external beauty.

## *You're On*

*1.* How do you really feel about the way you look?

*2.* If you do not feel good, take some time now to think about your relationship with God. Are you getting your worth and identity from Him? Once you do, you will begin to realize how beautiful you are. If you don't feel that, pray and ask Him to show you how He sees you.

*The greater part of your beauty cannot be bought, taken off a rack, applied like lipstick, or put on like a hat. The greater part of your attractiveness lies within; it wells up from the inside and finds an appropriate creative expression on the outside.*[2]

*3.* What are three non-physical things that are extra-special about you and that help you know how God looks at you?

*4.* What can you do in your spiritual life to complement your natural beauty? Remember, radiance starts on the inside. Peace and joy and gratitude will reveal themselves on your face.

## Learn Your Lines

*They looked to Him and were radiant,*
*and their faces were not ashamed.*
**Psalm 34:5**

*And let the beauty of the Lord our God be upon us . . .*
**Psalm 90:17a**

*I will praise you, for I am fearfully and wonderfully made;*
*marvelous are Your works, and that my soul knows very well.*
**Psalm 139:14**

*For the Lord takes pleasure in His people;*
*He will beautify the humble with salvation.*
**Psalm 149:4**

### Act 2: Hair, Skin, Nails, and Make-up

There are at least four areas that are crucial to looking your best: your hair (that's your glory, you know!) your skin, your nails, and your makeup. Beauty professionals can custom-make the look that's right for you in each of these areas, but listed below are several tips that apply to everyone.

Invest in a great haircut and learn how to maintain it (to style it yourself and to recognize when it's time to head back to the salon). It's funny, great haircuts are like great food: you can pay lots of money to get them in an elegant atmosphere, but you can also get a fabulous cut for $25 in a place that looks like a dive! The important thing is to find a stylist who is part good listener and part artist. Find someone who understands who you are and what your life is about and who has the ability to translate that to your head! Don't try to go about your grown-up business with high school hair!

Have a professional makeover as often as you can afford to. Your made-up face is the one the world sees, so you want to make sure your makeup is current (not dated) and that you know how to apply it as you age.

Have your nails done as often as possible. Not only is a manicure a relaxing treat, it ensures that your hands and nails will be attractive and well-groomed. I know one woman who found a nail color that worked so well on her that it became part of her signature look—you might consider that too!

You've heard before that the skin is the largest organ of the human body. Skin looks best when it is smooth and silky. Whether we are talking about your arms, your legs, or the bottoms of your feet, the key to silky skin is to moisturize, moisturize, moisturize. Remember that no man wants to crawl in bed with a crocodile!

The skin on your face requires extra care. Understand what type of skin you have and how to take care of it. If you don't know, ask a salesperson at the cosmetics counter of your choosing. Pay particular attention to the skin around your eyes, which wrinkles more quickly than other places on your face.

> *A beautiful girl is a natural wonder; a beautiful woman is a work of art.*
> **Anonymous**

## *You're On*

*1.* When was the last time you changed your hairstyle? Does your current style reflect your personality, your position in life and your age? No one wants to see a full-grown woman with junior-high hair!

### Tips
### for Lasting
### Lip Color

*1. Keep lips smooth and conditioned by regularly using lip balm.*

*2. Fill in entire lip with lipliner, then apply lipstick over the pencil to make color more durable.*

*3. When applied from a tube, lipstick just sits on top of lips. Use a lip brush to help color penetrate lips.*

*4. Choose a matte or semigloss formula; glossy finishes tend to have less staying power.*

*5. Blot with a tissue to remove excess and set the look.*[5]

*2.* Does your look tell the world that you are a leading lady? If not, what needs to change?

*3.* Take a look at your nails. Do they need attention? If so, get thee to the manicurist! If you cannot afford a regular manicure, get one as often as you can in order to keep your nails in shape. Then, between appointments, apply a base coat and some neutral polish to add a bit of shine.

*4.* Is it time for a makeover or are you convinced that the makeup you currently use is working for you?

# Learn Your Lines

*Do not let your adornment be merely outward—arranging the hair, wearing gold, or putting on fine apparel—rather let it be the hidden person of the heart, with the incorruptible beauty of a gentle and quiet spirit, which is very precious in the sight of God.*

**1 Peter 3:3, 4**

*Charm is deceitful and beauty is passing, but a woman who fears the Lord, she shall be praised.*

**Proverbs 31:30**

*The silver-haired head is a crown of glory, if it is found in the way of righteousness.*

**Proverbs 16:31**

## Act 3: A Wardrobe That Works

We know that clothes do not make the woman, but they certainly have a way of communicating about her! It is important for you to have a wardrobe befitting a leading lady and I want to offer some suggestions to help you get there.

Start by evaluating what you already have. Get in your closet and be brutal. Take stock of what you have. Some people say that you should get rid of anything you have not worn in the past year and others say two years. You make that decision; I'll present seven questions to ask yourself as you clean out your closet.

*1.* Does it reflect the woman that I am today?

*2.* Does it fit?

*3.* Is it worn, frayed, or pilled?

*4.* Is it in style?

*5.* Does it coordinate well with what I already have?

*6.* Do I feel confident in it?

*7.* Is it attractive while being appropriately modest? (This is especially true for business attire.)

Make sure your shoes are clean and polished and the heels are not worn or have frayed edges. Make sure they are not scuffed or scratched. Make an investment in a well-fitting, good-looking pair of shoes you can wear with a variety of outfits.

Find your signature. Whether it is a designer handbag, a strand of pearls like Jackie O., a certain nail color, or the perfect eyeglasses, find something you can wear often that really makes a statement about who you are. Don't forget to find a signature fragrance as well—but don't overdo it!

In many places, three-season fabrics work well—lightweight wools, gabardine, silks, and some cottons. Invest in suits that are made in these fabrics, especially lightweight wools and gabardines, so you can buy higher quality clothing that will look great most or all of the year. Choose your colors carefully so that you can move from winter to spring with ease by just changing your blouse and your accessories. With a crisp white blouse and a

> *Choose your [suit] colors carefully so that you can move from winter to spring with ease by just changing your blouse and your accessories.*

brightly colored scarf, that black suit will be as appropriate in May as it was with a turtleneck and boots in October!

Lady, may I be frank? Those garments called "foundations" or "underwear" are well-named. Your lingerie needs to stay *under* what you *wear*. Just like the foundation of a house, it exists to serve the purpose of supporting and protecting you—not for the purpose of being seen by the world. Keep your straps on your shoulders; keep your slip under your dress; and by all means do not allow the waistband of your briefs or bikinis to show when you bend over!

Have a good all-purpose coat that reflects your personal style. It's hard to go wrong with a classic trench coat in a classic color, but there are many other options, so find the one that's right for you.

## *You're On*

*1.* What is your top-ten "outta here" list? Come on, what are the ten things that need to be evicted from your closet without delay?

*2.* What is the one article of clothing you need to purchase first—the one that would coordinate with and update several things you already have?

*3.* What is the one accessory you need to purchase first—maybe a quality handbag, a stunning scarf, a piece of jewelry?

*4.* Which of your shoes do you need to polish or replace?

*5.* Check your foundations. What do you need to purchase in order to look good under your clothes?

## *Learn Your Lines*

*She makes tapestry for herself; her clothing is fine linen and purple.*

**Proverbs 31:22**

*But put on the Lord Jesus Christ . . . and make no provision for the flesh, to fulfill its lusts.*

**Romans 13:14**

*Therefore take up the whole armor of God, that you may be able to withstand in the evil day, and having done all, to stand. Stand therefore, having girded your waist with truth, having put on the breastplate of righteousness, and having shod your feet with the preparation of the gospel of peace; above all taking the shield of faith with which you will be able to quench all the fiery darts of the wicked one.*

**Ephesians 6:13–16**

# COMING SOON

$\mathcal{D}$o you ever look in the mirror and think about what you need to change about your clothes, your hair, your make-up, or some other aspect of your appearance? The way you look is a reflection of who you are. What kind of woman are you, and how can she be reflected in the way you look? Dream for a minute about "having it all together" in the area of grooming and appearance, and write down what kind of image you need to portray in order to accurately represent the excellence within you.

_____

_____

_____

_____

_____

_____

_____

_____

_____

_____

_____

_____

# ACTION!

*B*ased on what you have learned in this chapter, what are three concise, measurable, attainable goals you will set for yourself in terms of your appearance? Be sure to include a schedule and target date for reaching each goal and a reward for accomplishing it.

*1.* Goal:
Schedule and target completion date:
Reward:

*2.* Goal:
Schedule and target completion date:
Reward:

*3.* Goal:
Schedule and target completion date:
Reward:

# Appendix A: Goals at a Glance

Review the goals you set for yourself at the end of each chapter and compile them on the following pages. Keep them grouped the way they are grouped in the workbook, but put a star beside, a circle around, or some highlighting on the one that is most important to you out of each group. This will help you set your priorities. You might want to consider keeping that short list in your appointment book, daily calendar, or posting it on your refrigerator.

Chapter 1    1. _____    2. _____    3. _____

Chapter 2    1. _____    2. _____    3. _____

Chapter 3    1. _____    2. _____    3. _____

Chapter 4    1. _____    2. _____    3. _____

Chapter 5    1. _____    2. _____    3. _____

Chapter 6    1. _____    2. _____    3. _____

Chapter 7    1. _____    2. _____    3. _____

Chapter 8    1. _____    2. _____    3. _____

Chapter 9    1. _____    2. _____    3. _____

Chapter 11   1. _____    2. _____    3. _____

Chapter 12   1. _____    2. _____    3. _____

Chapter 13   1. _____    2. _____    3. _____

Chapter 14   1. _____    2. _____    3. _____

Chapter 15   1. _____    2. _____    3. _____

Chapter 16   1. _____    2. _____    3. _____

Chapter 17   1. _____    2. _____    3. _____

# Appendix B: The Lady's Budget

*This excellent basic budget worksheet is taken from Deborah Owens' book*
Confident Investing, *pages 259–262.*

## BASIC EXPENSES

| ITEM | WEEKLY | MONTHLY | YEARLY |
|---|---|---|---|
| **HOME EXPENSES** | | | |
| mortgage/rent  *PITI* | | | |
| real estate taxes | | | |
| ~~special assessment~~ | | | |
| home-equity loan | | | |
| **SECOND HOME EXPENSES** | | | |
| ~~mortgage~~ | | | |
| ~~real estate taxes~~ | | | |
| other expenses  *Worldmark* | | *64.88* | |
| ~~**APARTMENT EXPENSES**~~ | | | |
| ~~rent~~ | | | |
| ~~parking fees~~ | | | |
| ~~other fees~~ | | | |
| **GROUNDS MAINTENANCE** | | | |
| lawn service | | | |
| rubbish removal | | | |
| snow removal | | | |
| supplies/equipment | | | |
| tree and shrub care | | | |
| other | | | |
| **UTILITIES** | | | |
| electric | | | |
| water | | | |
| oil | | | |
| telephone | | | |
| gas | | | |
| ~~**INSURANCE**~~  *Mutual Fund* | | | |
| ~~homeowners~~  *Roth* | | | |
| ~~umbrella~~ | | | |
| **HOUSEHOLD** | | | |
| groceries | | | |
| cleaning supplies, etc. | | | |
| **CLOTHING** | | | |
| family | | | |
| dry cleaning | | | |
| **HEALTHCARE** | | | |
| insurance | | *Benefit* | *$460 Tricare* |
| doctor | | | |

| ITEM | WEEKLY | MONTHLY | YEARLY |
|---|---|---|---|
| prescriptions/medications | | | |
| dentist | | | |
| other | | | |
| **AUTO EXPENSES** | | | |
| loan payment | | | |
| gasoline | | | |
| repairs/maintenance | | | |
| insurance | | | |
| registration, license, etc. | | | |
| tolls | | | |
| parking | | | |
| other | | | |
| **TRANSPORTATION** | | | |
| bus, train, subway | | | |
| **LIFE INSURANCE PREMIUMS** | | | |
| policy 1 | | | |
| policy 2   *Unum Longterm care,* | | | |
| **DISABILITY INSURANCE PREMIUMS** | | | |
| policy 1 | | | |
| **ALIMONY AND CHILD SUPPORT** | | | |
| alimony | | | |
| child support | | | |
| **WORK RELATED** | | | |
| union dues | | | |
| continuing ed. | | | |
| other | | | |
| **CHILDCARE** | | | |
| daycare | | | |
| miscellaneous | | | |
| bank charge | | | |
| postage | | | |
| tax prep., legal | | | |
| other | | | |

If you have debts to pay, consult the debt-elimination worksheet in Appendix C and factor your bill payments into your budget.

**Total weekly expenses:** _____

**Total monthly expenses:** _____

**Total yearly expenses:** _____

# Appendix C: Eliminating Debt

This debt-elimination worksheet is adapted from Dave Ramsey's "Debt Snowball," which can be found on page 133 of his book, *Priceless*. He suggests listing your debts on this sheet from smallest to largest. Make minimum payments on all but your smallest debt (no matter what the interest rates on others are) and pay off that amount first. Once you have paid that debt, apply what you had been paying on it to the next debt on this list, thereby using the "snowball" effect until all your debts are paid.

| DEBT AMOUNT | CREDITOR | MINIMUM PAYMENT | TARGET PAY-OFF DATE | DATE PAID OFF |
|---|---|---|---|---|
| | | | | |
| | | | | |
| | | | | |
| | | | | |
| | | | | |
| | | | | |
| | | | | |
| | | | | |
| | | | | |
| | | | | |
| | | | | |
| | | | | |
| | | | | |
| | | | | |
| | | | | |
| | | | | |
| | | | | |
| | | | | |
| | | | | |
| | | | | |

# Appendix D: Healthy Recipes for the Leading Lady

*All of these recipes (and more!) can be found in my book,*
Lay Aside the Weight, *on pages 129–174.*

## Good Morning Juice

Serves 2
Per serving: 200 calories, 0 fat grams

12 ounces papaya
4 cups orange juice
½ cup sugar or 2 envelopes non-caloric sugar substitute
½ pound ice
1 teaspoon lemon juice
Clean papaya. Puree in blender with other ingredients. Drink within five minutes to receive full nutritional value.

## Banana Pancakes

Serves 12
Per serving: 220 calories, 3 fat grams

1 banana
1 teaspoon vanilla
½ cup orange juice
1 cup sugar
½ cup all purpose flour
½ cup coconut
1 teaspoon baking powder
½ teaspoon salt
4 egg whites, beaten until stiff
½ cup dried fruit
Puree banana, vanilla, and orange juice. Sift sugar, flour, coconut, baking powder, and salt in a bowl. Stir in banana mixture, egg whites, and dried fruit. Pour into pan and bake at 350° for 35 minutes.

## TNU3 Sandwich

Serves 4
Per serving: 275 calories, 5 fat grams

8 low-calorie bread slices
4 low-fat cheese slices
8 slices fat-free ham
4 teaspoons fat-free mayonnaise
4 slices avocado
4 slices onion
4 slices green pepper
4 slices tomato
1 package alfalfa sprouts
mustard
Toast bread. Make sandwich with one cheese slice between two slices of ham. Add remaining ingredients.

## Potato Salad

Serves 4
Per serving: 130 calories, 0 fat grams

4 boiled Idaho potatoes, cubed
3 boiled eggs, diced
4 teaspoons sweet pickle relish
1 cup diced celery
½ cup diced white onion
1 cup diced cucumber
2 teaspoons brown sugar
5 teaspoons fat-free mayonnaise
2 teaspoons fat-free ranch dressing
3 teaspoons mustard
Mix all the ingredients in a bowl.

## Turkey Fajitas

Serves: 4
Per serving: 410 calories, 3 fat grams

1 can fat-free refried beans
1 onion, sliced
1 green pepper, sliced
1 tomato, diced
1 fat-free smoked turkey breast, cut into strips
8 fat-free tortillas
½ cup salsa
½ cup fat-free cream
Heat refried beans. Saute onion and pepper until tender. Add tomato and turkey. Warm tortillas, fill them with turkey, and roll up. Serve with salsa, a spoonful of cream, and beans on the side.

## Cuban Yogurt

Serves 2
Per serving: 300 calories, 0 fat grams

1 cup skim milk
1 shot espresso coffee
2 teaspoons sugar or 1 envelope non-caloric sugar substitute
2 teaspoons fat-free chocolate syrup
6 cups fat-free vanilla yogurt
1 teaspoon cinnamon
In blender combine milk, espresso coffee, and sugar or non-caloric sugar substitute. Blend in chocolate syrup and yogurt on maximum speed till foam appears. Serve sprinkled with cinnamon on top.

## Cheesecake

Serves 12
Per serving: 400 calories, 3 fat grams

24 ounces fat-free cream cheese, room temperature
16 ounces fat-free cream
1 cup sugar
1 teaspoon vanilla
nonfat, nonstick spray
1 cup graham cracker crumbs

Meringue
6 egg whites
3 teaspoons sugar
1 teaspoon vanilla

Combine and beat on low speed cream cheese, cream, sugar, and vanilla. Be careful not to beat too long. Spray pie plate with nonfat, nonstick spray and press graham cracker crumbs into a crust. Pour in cream cheese mixture. Bake at 325° for 45 minutes or until pie is puffed up in the middle. Meringue: Beat egg whites until stiff. Combine sugar and vanilla and fold into egg whites. Pour on pie and bake 5 to 7 minutes. Let pie cool, then refrigerate for at least 2 hours before serving.

# NOTES

## Chapter 4

1. Nelson, Tommy. *The Book of Romance* (Nashville, TN: Thomas Nelson, Inc. 1998), 71.

## Chapter 5

1. Meyer, Joyce. *A Leader in the Making* (Tulsa, OK: Harrison House, 2001), 241.
2. Cloud, Dr. Henry and Dr. John Townsend. *Boundaries* (Grand Rapids, MI: Zondervan Publishing House, 1992), 149.
3. Ibid., 280.

## Chapter 6

1. T.D. Jakes, ed. *Holy Bible, Woman Thou Art Loosed Edition* (Nashville, TN: Thomas Nelson, Inc. 1998), 1329.
2. Ibid.
3. Ibid.
4. Ibid.

## Chapter 8

1. *A Leader in the Making*, 8.
2. Paula White, on *The Potter's Touch* television broadcast.

## Chapter 9

1. Henry Fielding in *Priceless*, (Nashville, TN: J. Countryman®, a division of Thomas Nelson, Inc.) 95.
2. J.W. Fulbright in *Priceless*, 38.
3. Ramsey, Dave in *Priceless*, 115.

## Chapter 10

1. McNaughton, Deborah. *Financially Secure* (Nashville, TN: Thomas Nelson, Inc., 2002), 63-64.
2. Ibid., 64-65
3. Owens, Deborah, *Confident Investing* (Indianapolis, IN: Alpha Books, 2001), 281.
4. Ibid., 270.
5. *USA Today* in *Priceless*, 90.
6. *Financially Secure*, 50.
7. Ibid., 51.
8. Ibid., 52.
9. Ibid.
10. Ibid., 61.
11. *Priceless*, 106.

## Chapter 11

1. *Confident Investing*, 7.
2. Ibid.,
3. Ibid., 7-8.
4. Ibid., 8.
5. Ibid.
6. Ibid.
7. Ibid.
8. Ibid.
9. Ibid., 61.

## Chapter 12

1. *Confident Investing*, 226.
2. Ibid.
3. Ibid.
4. Ibid.
5. Ibid.
6. Wallace, Curtis W., ed. *In the Multitude of Counsel* (Dallas, TX: T.D. Jakes Enterprises, 2001), 248-249.
7. *Confident Investing*, 228.
8. Ibid.
9. Ibid., 235
10. Ibid.
11. Ibid., 23

## Chapter 13

1. *Financially Secure*, 193.
2. Ibid.
3. Ibid.
4. Ibid.
5. Ibid., 193-194.
6. Ibid., 194.
7. Ibid., 184-185.
8. Ibid., 186.
9. Ibid., 186-187.
10. Ibid., 189.
11. Ibid., 182.
12. Ibid., 190.

## Chapter 14

1. Jakes, T.D. *Lay Aside the Weight* (Tulsa, OK: Albury Publishing, 1997), 121.
2. Peg Rosen. "Six Ways to Live Longer and Happier." *Good Housekeeping* (June 2002), 54.
3. Peter Flax. "Fast Food Now." *Reader's Digest* (November 2002), 77.

4. Savage, Gary, Tony Jarvis and Sarah J. Henry. *The Little Blue Book of Fitness and Health* (Nashville, TN: Rutledge Hill Press, 1998).
5. *Reader's Digest*, 79.
6. Pythagoras in *Lay Aside the Weight*, 24.
7. *Lay Aside the Weight*, 66.
8. Food Truths are from *Lay Aside the Weight*, 77-79.
9. Ibid., 124.
10. Ibid., 30.

## Chapter 15

1. Semler, Tracy Chutorian. *All About Eve.* revised and updated. (Nashville, TN: Rutledge Hill Press, 1995, 2001).
2. Ibid., 453-454.
3. Ibid., 460.
4. Ibid.
5. Ibid., 455.
6. Ibid., 461.
7. Ibid., 460.
8. Ibid., 461-462.
9. Ibid., 461.
10. Ibid., 457.
11. Ibid., 458.
12. Ibid, 334.
13. Ibid.,355.
14. Ibid.
15. Ibid., 352.
16. Ibid.
17. Ibid., 337.
18. Ibid., 351.

## Chapter 16

1. *Lay Aside the Weight*, 29-30.
2. Ibid., 86.
3. Ibid., 72.
4. *The Little Blue Book of Fitness and Health*, #72.
5. *Lay Aside the Weight*, 82.

## Chapter 17

1. *Holy Bible, Woman Thou Art Loosed Edition*, 1359.
2. Ibid.
3. Gordon Espinet, *Good Housekeeping* (July 2002), 23.